Salvador Mafé Hu

Dessault Mirage F1s

in Ejército del Aire service

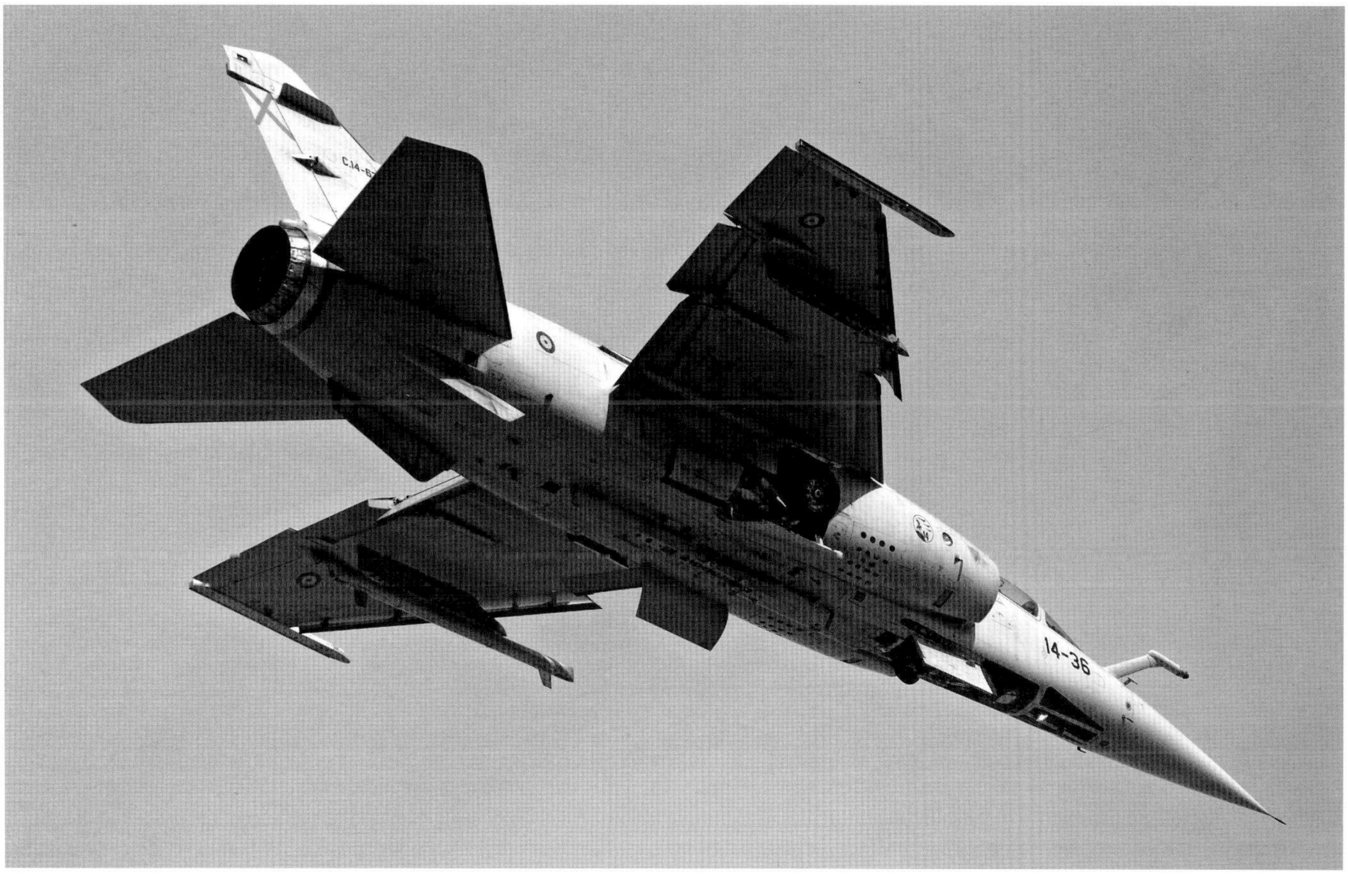

Dedicated to my good and dear friend during so many years Rafael Treviño Martínez, always supportive.

MORE FROM KAGERO

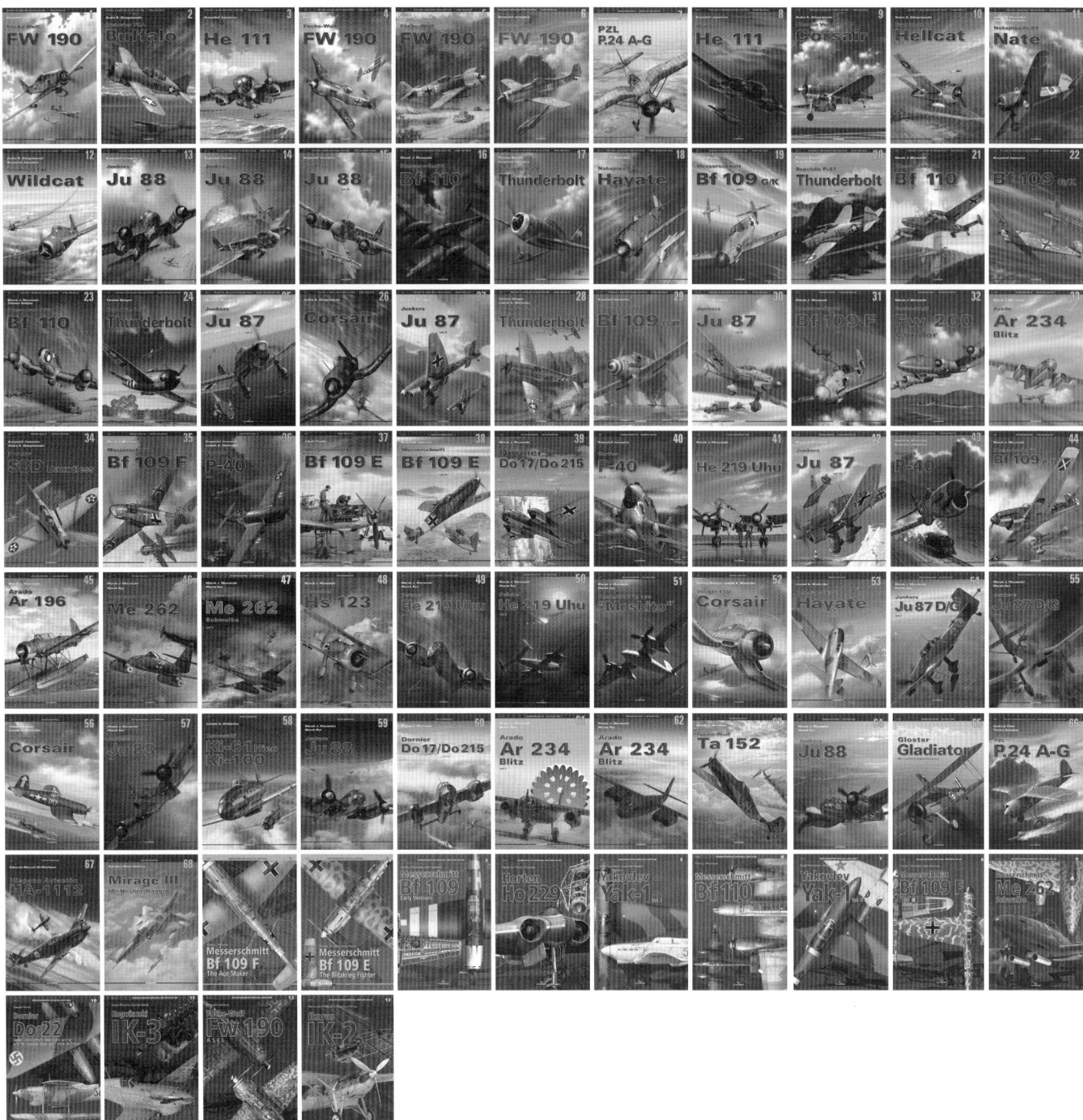

www.shop.kagero.pl • phone + 4881 5012105

Dessault Mirage F1s • Salvador Mafé Huertas • First edition • LUBLIN 2020

© All rights reserved. With the exception of quoting brief passages for the purposes of review, no part of this publication may be reproduced without prior written permission from the Publisher. Nazwa serii zastrzeżona w UP RP • ISBN 978-83-66148-81-9

Editing: **Salvador Mafé Huertas** • Translation: **Salvador Mafé Huertas** • Color profiles: **Anastasios Polychronis** • Photos: **Dassault, S. Mafé, Juanjo Fernández, José Manuel Santaner Bosch, Ala 14, Tono Fernández Leonarte, Rafael Treviño Martínez, Juanma Vila, Ala 46** • Design: **KAGERO STUDIO – Łukasz Maj**
• Printed in Poland

KAGERO Publishing
Akacjowa 100, Turka, os. Borek, 20-258 Lublin 62, Poland, phone/fax: (+48) 81 501 21 05
www.kagero.pl • e-mail: kagero@kagero.pl, marketing@kagero.pl
w w w . k a g e r o . p l
Distribution: **KAGERO Publishing**

Acknowledgements

The Spanish Air Force was the second Mirage F1 customer, and purchased a total of 91 machines of different variants. From here I would like to appreciate very much to all the people who contributed in one form or another to this book: My friends Rafael Treviño Martínez, Juan José Fernández Martín, José Manuel Santaner Bosch, Juan Antonio Guerrero Misa, the late Javier Valero Soria and Javier Gómez Matute. At the Public Affairs Office of the Spanish Air Force HQ, to all the Commanding Officers of Ala 11, Ala 14 and Ala 46, to all its pilots and maintainers, especially to the whole 111 Escuadrón (while equipped with the Mirage F1), to Fernando Caballero de Pro, Joaquín Sánchez Díaz, Manuel Abadía, José María Salom Piqueres, Juan Carlos Raimundo, César Lardíes, Rafael Nuñez González, Jorge Albalat Estela, Chemi Quintana, Tono Fernández Leonarte, Jorge Portalés Alberola, Carlos Parallé Lorente and Manuel Rosa Bueno; my apologies if I forgot somebody…

Ala 14, Escuadrones 141 & 142

The Mirage F1 emerged from a series of design studies performed by French aircraft manufacturer Dassault Aviation. Having originally sought to develop a larger swept wing derivative of the Mirage III, which became the Mirage F2, to serve as a vertical take-off and landing (VTOL) propulsion testbed akin to the Dassault Mirage IIIV, however, it was soon recognised that the emerging design could function as the basis for a competent fighter as well. Both the Mirage F2 and a smaller derivative, referred to the Mirage F3, received substantial attention from both Dassault and the French Air Force, the latter being interested in its adoption as a long-range fighter bomber as a stopgap measure prior to the adoption of the envisioned Anglo-French Variable Geometry (AFVG) strike aircraft.

Parallel with the Mirage F3 study, which was intended to serve as an interceptor aircraft, Dassault decided to study a single-seat derivative which featured the all-French SNECMA Atar 9K-50 turbojet engine. As a result of the cancellation of two major projects, the company's design team found themselves with a decreased workload. Accordingly, in mid-1964, Dassault decided to commence design work on the smaller aircraft, subsequently designated as the Mirage F1, with the intention of producing a successor to its Mirage III and Mirage 5 fighters; This work was performed under a government contract in anticipation of a potential French Air Force specification for an all-weather interceptor to succeed its fleet of Mirage IIIC aircraft.

The Mirage F1 was of similar size to the delta-winged Mirage III and Mirage 5, and was powered by the same SNECMA Atar engine as had been used on the larger Dassault Mirage IV; however, unlike its predecessors, it shared the layout of a swept wing mounted high on the fuselage and a conventional tail surface as used

The two seat strike Mirage F2. [Dassault]

The varable geometry Mirage G8. [Dassault]

First prototype of the Mirage F1. [Dassault]

Another view of the Mirage F2 two seat strike jet. [Dassault]

countering flutter, killing its pilot. Despite this misfortune, during late 1966, the Mirage F1 programme was officially adopted by the French Air Force. Following a redesign period, on 20 March 1967, the second prototype performed its first flight.

On 26 May 1967, an order for three Mirage F1 prototypes was placed, while the larger and more expensive Mirage F2 was formally abandoned. These three pre-service aircraft, along with a static structural test airframe, soon joined the test programme. By late 1971, the construction of an initial batch of 85 production standard Mirage F1 had been authorised.

In order to comply with the French Air Force's requirement for an all-weather interceptor, the first production Mirage F1C was equipped with a Thomson-CSF Cyrano IV radar system. The later Cyrano IV-1 version added a limited look-down capability. However, Mirage F1 pilots reported that the radar was prone to overheating, which reduced its efficiency.[citation needed] During May 1973, the first deliveries to the French Air Force took place; the type entered squadron service with EC 2/30 Normandie-Niemen in December of that year.

By October 1971, the Mirage F1 was under production at both Dassault's Bordeaux facility and at SABCA's own plant in Belgium, work at the latter having been performed under an industrial arrangement associated to Belgium's order for 106 Mirage 5 aircraft. The 79 aircraft of the next production run were delivered during the period March 1977 to December 1983. These were of the Mirage F1C-200 version, which featured a fixed refuelling probe, which required an extension of the fuselage by 7 cm.

The Dassault Mirage F1 was a single-engine fighter aircraft, designed to function as both an interceptor aircraft and as a capable ground attack platform. While officially developed for the French Air Force as a capable air defense aircraft, Dassault had placed considerable em-

by the F2. Although it has a smaller wingspan than the Mirage III, the Mirage F1 nevertheless proved to be superior to its predecessor, carrying more fuel while possessing a shorter take-off run and superior maneuverability.

On 23 December 1966, the first prototype conducted its maiden flight. The first flight had been delayed due to a funding shortage affecting the overall programme. During its fourth flight, the prototype was recorded as having attained a top speed in excess of Mach 2. On 18 May 1967, the first prototype was lost in an accident at DGA Essais en vol, Istres; the crash had resulted from a loss of control after en-

Prototype of the Super Mirage F1, fitted with the M53 engine, if series production could have proceded, the aircraft could have been quite different. [Dassault]

phasis on developing the Mirage F1 for ground attack duties as a secondary role during its early design. Developed by the company to function as a successor to the successful Mirage III and Mirage 5 families, it drew heavily upon its predecessors as well, sharing the same fuselage as the Mirage III, while adopting a considerably different wing configuration.

The Mirage F1 used a shoulder-mounted swept wing, instead of the Delta wing of the Mirage III, which resulted in a more than 50% reduction in required runway lengths and increased internal fuel tankage for 40% greater combat range. The approach speed prior to landing is 25% less than the preceding Mirage IIIE. According to Dassault, the negative performance impact associated with the increased thickness of the Mirage F1's wing over the Mirage III's counterpart had been offset by improvements made to the propulsion system. The wing is fitted with both double-slotted trailing edge flaps and full-span leading edge slats, the latter being automatically operated to reduce the aircraft's turn radius during combat.

The Dassault Mirage F1 was designed to replace the successful Dassault Mirage III series. The aircraft was designed for high-speed handling with low and high-altitude performance, multi-faceted capabilities in the fighter or strike aircraft role and to provide the pilot with some minor conveniences for long sorties requiring short turnaround times. Over 720 Mirage F1 examples have been produced. The F1 remained until its withdrawal from service (except perhaps Iran) one of the most battle-tested aircraft systems of the Cold War. [S. Mafé]

F1M C.14-70 was subject to the 100th Mirage F1 general overhaul at the Albacete Maintenance Centre in 2005, thus its tail markings, and its insignia. [Juanjo Fernández]

A key area of advancement on the Mirage F1 over its predecessors was in its onboard avionics. The Thomson-CSF Cyrano IV monopulse radar system, developed from the Cyrano II unit installed on the Mirage IIIE, serves as the main sensor; it operates in three different modes: air-target acquisition and tracking, ground mapping, and terrain avoidance. The later Cyrano IV-1 model also provided for a limited lookdown capability. According to aerospace publication Flight International, the Cyrano IV radar was capable of detecting aerial targets at double the range of earlier models. The standard production Mirage F1 was furnished with an Instrument Landing System (ILS), radar altimeter, UHF/VHF radio sets, Tactical Air Navigation system (TACAN) and aground data link. Other avionics include an autopilot and yaw damper.

The Mirage F1 was powered by a single SNECMA Atar 9K-50 turbojet engine, which was capable of providing roughly 7 tonnes-force (69 kN; 15,000 pounds) of thrust, giving the aircraft a maximum speed of 1,453 MPH and an altitude ceiling of 65,615 feet. Flight International described the Atar engine as being "unexpectedly simple", despite the adoption

Almost since Ala 14 comissioning in 1975, it regularly deployed about six times per year to Son San Juan air base, in Majorca Island, ideally located for controlling the western Mediterranean. [José Manuel Santaner Bosch]

of an afterburner. An improved engine, initially known as the Super Atar and later as the Snecma M53, was intended to be eventually adopted on production Mirage F1 aircraft, as well as for successor aircraft.

The initial armament of the Mirage F1 was a pair of internal 30 mm cannons, and a single Matra R530 medium-range air-to-air missile, which was carried under the fuselage. It could carry a total combined payload of 13,889lb

Ala 14, Escuadrones 141 & 142

During 2003, Ala 14, spent two one week detachments a Gioia del Colle air base in southern Italy, patrolling the skies over the troubled former Jugoslavia, almost two years after the Spanish Air Force EF-18 Hornets ceased their operations from Aviano air base. [Ala 14]

141 Escuadrón F1Ms during an exchange with the Aeronautica Militare Italiana. [Ala 14]

Ala 14, Escuadrones 141 & 142

In June 1975, with tension growing with Morocco, Spain decided to strengthen its Air Force and bought 15 Mirage F1CE that were allocated to Albacete AB. In mid-1976 there was still some tension with Morocco and Algerian and Libyan MiG-25 flights on the Mediterranean, which would lead the Spanish Air Force to purchase ten more Mirage F1C and two years later order 48 Mirage F1CE and F1EE. [S. Mafé]

quested the integration of the Sidewinder upon their own Mirage F1CE and Mirage F1CG fighters.

In June 1975, with tension growing with Morocco, Spain decided to strengthen its Air Force and bought 15 Mirage F1CE that were allocated to Albacete AB. In mid-1976 there was still some tension with Morocco and Algerian and Libyan MiG-25 flights on the Mediterranean, which would lead the Spanish Air Force to purchase ten more Mirage F1C and two years later order 48 Mirage F1CE and F1EE.

141 pilots at Amendola air base, Italy. [Ala 14]

Briefing prior to a mission (left photo). Getting dressed with the anti-g, and the survival vest (right photo). [S. Mafe]

of bombs and missiles, all of which would be carried externally. After 1979, the medium-range R530 was replaced by the improved Super 530F missile as the latter came into service in quantity with the French Air Force. In 1977, the R550 Magic was released; the Mirage F1 has these missiles mounted on rails on the wingtips. Around the same time, the American AIM-9 Sidewinder was also introduced to the Mirage F1's armament; both the Spanish and Hellenic Air Forces had re-

Some years later Spain also bought 12 F1E-DA/DDA's retired from Qatar Air Force, which also sold some equipment and weapons used by those Mirage F1s. In Spanish service the F1CE was known as the C.14A, the F1EE was the C.14B, the two-seater as CE.14 and the F1EDA/DDA as the C.14C/CE.14C

They served mainly as Spain's primary air defence interceptors and interdiction as secondary role until they were superseded by

Ala 14, Escuadrones 141 & 142

Since the Baltic States, Estonia, Latvia and Lithuania are part of the NATO, the air defence of these states is the responsibility of the other NATO members. The mission is called Baltic Air Policing and since March 2004 the alliance nations of NATO have policed the Baltic airspace on a three or four month rotation. On the 1st of August 2006 Spain took over the patrol missions from Turkey. Four Mirage F1Ms transferred to Siauliai Air Base in Lithuania together with more then 80 servicemen. The pilots of Ala 14 scrambled thrice to intercept undisclosed intruders until the mission was taken over by the Belgians on the 1st of December 2006. [Ala 14]

Since the Baltic States, Estonia, Latvia and Lithuania are part of the NATO, the air defence of these states is the responsibility of the other NATO members. The mission is called Baltic Air Policing and since March 2004 the alliance nations of NATO have policed the Baltic airspace on a three or four month rotation. On the 1st of August 2006 Spain took over the patrol missions from Turkey. Four Mirage F1Ms transferred to Siauliai Air Base in Lithuania together with more then 80 servicemen. The pilots of Ala 14 scrambled thrice to intercept undisclosed intruders until the mission was taken over by the Belgians on the 1st of December 2006. [Ala 14]

Spain's EF-18A Hornets. They served with Ala 11 in Manises (Ex-Qatari planes), Ala 14 in Albacete, and Ala 46 at Gando in the Canary Islands. Ala 46 used their Mirage F1s mainly as air defence planes, using same deep blue color pattern as French planes.

In October 1996, Thomson-CSF (actually Thales) was awarded a FFr700 million (US$96m) contract to upgrade 48 F1CE/EE single-seaters and 4 F1EB trainers to Mirage F1M standard (see below). Ex-Qatar Mirage F1s were left outside the upgrade, as it was a different version, and were the first ones to be retired in 2002. As well as a service-life extension, this improved the avionics and added look down, terrain following capability with an upgraded Cyrano IVM radar.

Lt Col Del Cid (left) Ala 14 detachment Commander during the F1M BAP deployement. [Ala 14]

The Mirage F1 was powered by a single SNECMA Atar 9K-50 turbojet engine, which was capable of providing roughly 7 tonnes-force (69 kN; 15,000 pounds) of thrust, giving the aircraft a maximum speed of 1,453 MPH and an altitude ceiling of 65,615 feet. Flight International described the Atar engine as being "unexpectedly simple", despite the adoption of an afterburner. An improved engine, initially known as the Super Atar and later as the Snecma M53, was intended to be eventually adopted on production Mirage F1 aircraft, as well as for successor aircraft. [S. Mafé]

The upgrade for developed the two seat Mirage F1BM was minimum, and mainly consisted in the installation of the Spanish developed and built (by Indra) AN/ALR-300 radar warning & homing receiver, noticed by the squared antenas in the leading and training edges of the vertical fin. [S. Mafé]

The upgrade for the two seat Mirage F1BM was minimum, and mainly consisted in the installation of the Spanish developed and built (by Indra) AN/ALR-300 radar warning & homing receiver, noticed by the squared antenas in the leading and training edges of the vertical fin. [S. Mafé]

From July 2006 to November 2006, Spanish Mirage F1s were deployed to Lithuania as a part of NATO's Baltic Air Policing mission; during this deployment, they were scrambled twice to intercept undisclosed intruders. On 20 January 2009, a pair of Spanish F1s from Ala 14 collided in flight near their base during a routine dogfight training mission, resulting in the deaths of all three crew members, it was a single seat F1M and a two seat F1BM (see box with serials). The wreckage of the two jets, including the remains of the aircrew, was found about 3 km (1.9 mi) apart. By 2009, there were 38 F1M's in service with Escuadrón 141 "Patanes" and 142 Escuadrón "Tigres" of Ala 14.

In June 2013, the Spanish Air Force retired its fleet of Mirage F1s, having progressively phased the type out of service as increasing numbers of the Eurofighter Typhoon had become available. During 2013, it was reported that Spain could sell sixteen F1M's to Argentina but it seems they had the budget to buy new Kfirs instead, although neither of these possibilities materialized. The deal went through and Argentina bought the Spanish Mirages in October 2013, but the deal was scrapped in March 2014 after pressure from the United Kingdom on Spain to not assist in FAA modernization over tensions between the countries over the Falkland Islands. In November 2017, Draken International announced that it had acquired 20

Mirage F1BM being readied for a sortie inside one of Los Llanos HAS. [S. Mafé]

Juan Luis Abad Cellini was a Mirage F1 pilot from the first era, and in the years 2000/2002 returned as Ala 14 Commanding officer, having logged more than 3.000 flight hours in the French fighter; unfortunately as a Lt General and Commander of Air combat Command, died in June 2012 from a heart stroke. [S. Mafé]

After the Mirage F1 retirement, the tails of a jet of 141 and 142 Escuadrones adorn the entrance to Ala 14 operations building. [S. Mafé]

The Mirage F1s served mainly as Spain's primary air defence interceptors and interdiction as secondary role until they were superseded by Spain's EF-18A Hornets. They operated with Ala 11 in Manises (Ex-Qatari planes), Ala 14 in Albacete, and Ala 46 at Gando in the Canary Islands. Ala 46 used their Mirage F1s mainly as air defence planes, using same deep blue color pattern as French planes. In October 1996, Thomson-CSF was awarded a FFr700 million (US$96m) contract to upgrade 48 F1CE/EE single-seaters and 4 F1EB trainers to Mirage F1M standard (see below). Ex-Qatar Mirage F1s were left outside the upgrade, as it was a different version, and were the first ones to be retired in 2002. As well as a service-life extension, this improved the avionics and added look down, terrain following capability with a modernised Cyrano IVM radar. [S. Mafé]

F1Ms from Spain and would refurbish and upgrade them for use as adversary aircraft.

Although the Mirage F1 was withdrawn from use, just after accomplishing 37 years of stalwart service replaced completely by the Typhoon, but at the time of its retirement it was still capable of fullfilling its tasks - even to escort the King of Spain when he is flying out, or returning from a foreign visit. Thanks to its intensive modernization, the Mirage F1M was until retirement a very important asset in the fast jet force of Spain.

The Dassault Mirage F1 series was designed to replace the successful Dassault Mirage III se-

Ala 14, Escuadrones 141 & 142

Ala 14 Mirage F1Ms operating from Los Llanos-Albacete air base, southeast Spain during the mid-2000s. [Ala 14]

Underside view of a Mirage F1M, note the mock cockpit painted below the real one. [Ala 14]

Ala 14, Escuadrones 141 & 142

A clean Mirage F1M landing at Los Llanos-Albacete, what it lacked its Atar 09K50 of thrust, was gained by the excellent aerodinamics. [Juanjo Fernández]

A Mirage F1M taking off from Los llanos, it can be appreciated the rather complicated folding of the main landing gear. [S. Mafé]

ries. The aircraft was designed for high-speed handling with low and high-altitude performance, multi-faceted capabilities in the fighter or strike aircraft role and to provide the pilot with some minor conveniences for long sorties requiring short turnaround times. Over 720 Mirage F1 examples have been produced. The F1 remained until its withdrawal from service (except perhaps Iran) one of the most battle-tested aircraft systems of the Cold War. The first Mirage F1 prototype was completely funded by Dassault and flew for the first time on December 23rd, 1966. The French Air Force was pleased with the first results and selected the aircraft for further development in the form of additional prototypes in May 1967. The results of minor improvements to the airframe and the performance of the aircraft were satisfactory and the full operational status of the first production models was achieved in May 1973. The aircraft became a highly regarded interceptor - one of the best at the time of its inception - based on capabilities and its powerful nose-mounted radar. This system could track and engage multiple targets at any altitude. The interest of many air forces in this aircraft was a fact.

The Mirage F1 programme

The Ejército del Aire was the second air force to order the Mirage F1. Due to its central position in the mainland of Spain, a new wing

The Mirage F1Ms were retired from Ala 14 service in June 2013, replaced by the much more advanced Eurofighter Typhoon. [S. Mafé]

Ala 14, Escuadrones 141 & 142

A pair of Ala 14 Mirage F1Ms just before engaging the refueling hoses of an Ala 31 KC-130H Hercules. [Ala 14]

Tiger tails: the scheme applied to C.14-56 and C.14-64 for the Tiger Meet. [Tono Fernández Leonarte]

of the then Air Defence Command was commissioned on Base Aerea Los Llanos-Albacete to be equipped with the new Mirage F1 fighter.

The new wing; Ala 14, or more precisely 141 Escuadrón (squadron), received the first machine directly from Mont-de-Marsan in France and handed over on 18 June 1975. Soon after, the first squadron of Ala 14 was equipped with 16 Mirage F1CEs and became fully operational. Unfortunately the first one crashed on 4 January 1977. A further batch of aircraft equipped the already newly formed 142 Escuadrón from April 1980, and in October that same year the first two seater (Mirage F1BE) arrived. This wing focused their training on interception tasks and in January 1982 they reached the milestone of twenty five thousand flight hours. Not uncommon these days, the whole wing operated from flight lines in the open air but this changed when the first hardened shelters were built to accomodate the Mirage F1s in 1985. The multirole Mirage F1EEs were delivered from October 1981 until March 1983 and transferred to 462 Escuadrón as part of Ala 46 based at Gando-Las Palmas Air Base, in the Canary Islands.

The Spanish Mirage F1s were delivered from 1975 through 1983, with the machines obtained in three separate batches. In total 45 F1CEs, 22 F1EEs multi-role and 6 F1BE two-seaters were delivered. In the beginning, the F1Cs and F1EEs were designated C.14 and the F1BEs CE.14. The F1CEs and F1BEs were originally delivered with sand/brown/green camouflage topside and light gray underneath (also known as lizard scheme) while the F1EEs were delivered with medium blue on top and light gray on the bottom. The F1BEs assigned to Ala 14 received the same lizard camouflage as the F1CEs.

Due to a higher than expected attrition rate, the Ejército del Aire sought more airframes in the early 90s. Part of the solution came from Qatar since their Mirage F1s were in surplus as they favoured the new Mirage 2000-5. The first ex-Qatari Mirage F1 arrived in Spain on 23 Augusts 1994. In total, eleven single seaters (Mirage F1EDA) and two two seaters (Mirage F1DDA) were delivered to Spain until 1997.The Spanish realised that the airframes were in perfect condition and hence the Spanish put them in service immediately. They continued to maintain their two-tone brown and blue colour scheme, although when in service with Ala 14, some were painted in the standard grey overall. All Mirage F1EDAs and Mirage F1DDAs became operational in 111 Escuadrón of Ala 11 at Manises-Valencia Air Base, replac-

Ala 14, Escuadrones 141 & 142

The Ejército del Aire was the second air force to order the Mirage F1. Due to its central position in the mainland of Spain, a new wing of the then Air Defence Command was commissioned on Base Aerea Los Llanos-Albacete to be equipped with the new Mirage F1 fighter. The new wing; Ala 14, or more precisely 141 Escuadrón (squadron), received the first machine directly from Mont-de-Marsan in France and handed over on 18 June 1975. Soon after, the first squadron of Ala 14 was equipped with 16 Mirage F1CEs and became fully operational. Unfortunately the first one crashed on 4 January 1977. A further batch of aircraft equipped the already newly formed 142 Escuadrón from April 1980, and in October that same year the first two seater (Mirage F1BE) arrived. This wing focused their training on interception tasks and in January 1982 they reached the milestone of twenty five thousand flight hours. Not uncommon these days, the whole wing operated from flight lines in the open air but this changed when the first hardened shelters were built to accomodate the Mirage F1s in 1985. The multi-role Mirage F1EEs were delivered from October 1981 until March 1983 and transferred to 462 Escuadrón as part of Ala 46 based at Gando-Las Palmas Air Base, in the Canary Islands. [S. Mafé]

The first upgraded Mirage F1Ms arrived to Ala late in 1998. [S. Mafé]

Then Captain Pascual Soria, from 142 Escuadrón, before climbing into the narrow cockpit of a Mirage F1M. [S.Mafé]

Close-uo of "14-44" with Captain Pascual Soria ate the controls. [S. Mafé]

Los Lalnso air base tarmac, with some F1Ms in the flight line. [S. Mafé]

Ala 14, Escuadrones 141 & 142

A Mirage F1M (flown by José María Salom – then Ala 14 Operations Commander, and an F1EDA (flown by Major Juan Carlos Raimundo, the 142 Escuadrón C.O.) flying near the Peñón de Ifach in the province of Alicante, December 1999. [S. Mafé]

ing the loaned Mirage F1s of Ala 14. The same deal included additional engines, spare parts and 40 Matra Super 530 radar guided AAMs. More airframes came from the Armée de l'Air. One surplus two-seater and four single seaters delivered between November 1994 and March 1995 became part of Ala 14 and retained their medium blue camouflage until the midlife modernisation programme. But the life of the Mirage F1 at Ala 11 was limited. Manises-Valencia AB was to be closed due to budget cuts and relocation of assets so all the Mirage F1EDAs and DDAs were moved to Ala 14 by the end of September 1998. In total Spain received 91 Mirage F1 of four variants, and in the post F-86F Sabre, it was the second biggest fast jet fleet, only surpassed by the EF-18A/B, F/A-18A fleet, with 96 examples and closely followed by the C101EB Aviojet basic trainer with 88 examples.

From 2003, the Tactical Leadership Programme (TLP) was looking for a new air base with improved weather conditions and with less flight restrictions. Belgium demanded that the transfer would be from the then present Florennes airbase to another country, due to problems of air traffic congestion while the TLP demanded this transfer take place due to unstable weather conditions. In 2007 TLP announced that its new location was to be Albacete-Los Llanos, Spain. Since October 2009 the Mirages of Ala 14 have had to share the airbase and airspace with numerous participant of the TLP. On the other hand the TLP gives the pilots of Ala 14 the opportunity to take part of every edition of the TLP in order to gain more expertise and skills. Major Diego Caamaño states: "Since the TLP is around the corner it is easy the join the course at the last minute when the opportunity occurs".

Upgrading the fleet

During the late 80s and into the 90s the whole Mirage F1 fleet was standardised from the original lizard or blue colour scheme to the Celomer PU-66 NATO light grey scheme., except the nose radome which remained black, until a few years later that thse were painted grey also The paint was more resistant against corrosion, a false cockpit was painted underneath the real cockpit. Another change of the Mirage F1 fleet was the assembly of Tracor AN/ALE-40 Chaff/Flare dispensers being located under the horizontal stabilator on both sides of the fuselage, as well as the inddinegounsly developed and buil AN/ALR-300 RWR. The Air-to-Air missiles were upgraded from AIM-9N Sidewinders into AIM-9JULI, which included a seeker unit of the AIM-9L to give improved capabilities.

A key area of advancement on the Mirage F1 over its predecessors was in its onboard avionics. The Thomson-CSF Cyrano IV monopulse radar system, developed from the Cyrano II unit installed on the Mirage IIIE, serves as the main sensor; it operates in three different modes: air-target acquisition and tracking, ground mapping, and terrain avoidance. The later Cyrano IV-1 model also provided for a limited look-down capability. According to aerospace publication Flight International, the Cyrano IV radar was capable of detecting aerial targets at double the range of earlier models. The standard production Mirage F1 was furnished with an Instrument Landing System (ILS), radar altimeter, UHF/VHF radio sets, Tactical Air Navigation system (TACAN) and aground data link. Other avionics include an autopilot and yaw damper. [Rafael Treviño]

Ala 14, Escuadrones 141 & 142

A Mirage F1M flown by Lieutenant Colonel José María Salom – then Ala 14 Operations Commander, photographed near Los Llanos air base, in December 1999. [S. Mafé]

The Mirage F1 with is sleek lines, which can readily be appreciated in these images, served mainly as Spain's primary air defence interceptors and interdiction as secondary role until they were superseded by Spain's EF-18A Hornets. [S. Mafé]

Until the arrival of the EF-18 Hornet, the Mirage F1 was Spain's top fighter. After the introduction of the Hornet in 1986 the Mirage F1 still remained an important asset for air defence and ground attack. An avionics and service-life upgrading programme was investigated in the beginning of the 90s. Once the specifications of the programme were set, the modernisation contract, valued at US$96m, was awarded to Thomson-CSF RCM (now Thales Group) in October 1996. It covered a Service-Life Extension Programme (SLEP) and an avionics upgrade for 48 F1CE/EE single seaters and four F1BE (CE.14) two-seat trainers. Spanish companies like Amper Programas, Indra and CASA (the later now part of part of Airbus) acted as sub-contractors, together with ATE of South Africa. The latter was responsible for the design and integration of the navigation, display and weapons systems.

Apart from the SLEP, the upgrade package included a revised cockpit configuration with a multi purpose colour liquid crystal display and a Smart HUD from Sextant Avionique, now part of Thales as well. Another novelty was the Sextant Inertial Navigation System with GPS interface, NATO-compatible Have Quick 2 secure communications, Mode 4 digital IFF, a defensive aids suite, and flight recorders. The cockpit lighting became compatible for night vision

Ala 14, Escuadrones 141 & 142

The author in the Mirage F1M simulator, Los Llanos air base, November 2007. [S. Mafé]

On 23 June 2013, the Mirage F1s were officially retired from active service, being relieved by the Eurofighter Typhoon; first to equip was 142 Escuadrón, followed four years later (in 2017) by 141 Escuadrón. [Rafael Treviño Martínez]

On 23 June 2013, the Mirage F1s were officially retired from active service, being relieved by the Eurofighter Typhoon; first to equip was 142 Escuadrón, followed four years later (in 2017) by 141 Escuadrón. [Rafael Treviño Martínez]

Ala 14, Escuadrones 141 & 142

On Friday 8 September 2018 Draken International closed a deal with the Spanish Air Force, purchasing 20 Mirage F1 fighter aircraft. The supersonic F1s will complement Draken's existing fleet, which is currently flying on contract at Nellis AFB, Nev., supporting the Air Warfare Center. "Our mission is to provide the most cost effective solution to complement organic Red Air assets. We deliver a turnkey solution at a fraction of the cost the Air Force would spend generating the same number of sorties we produce everyday. Not only are we generating four to five sorties for the cost of a single F-16 flight hour, each flying hour preserves valuable life on USAF aircraft. Tremendous savings happen when squadrons are not tapped to go TDY away from their families to support Nellis with an already tiring deployment schedule," said Draken CEO Jared Isaacman. The Mirage F1s are projected to include a helmet mounted cueing system, infrared missile seekers, data link, and electronic jamming from its radar as well as radar warning receiver capabilities. [Tono Fernández]

Retired Mirage F1Ms and F1BMs awaiting to be dismantled and transported by sea to Draken International premises in Florida, US. [Tono Fernández]

The aggressive camouflage scheme which is being applied fot the ex Spanish AF Mirage F1Ms by Draken International. [Julio Maiz Sanz]

goggles and hands on throttle and stick (HOTAS) and some enhancements to the Cyrano IVM radar for accurate ground-attack and mapping capabilities in four different modes was implemented. The upgraded prototype of the Mirage was prepared by SABCA in Belgium and made its debut flight in April 1998. The remaining aircraft were modernised in Spain by CASA at Getafe (Madrid). The first upgraded Mirage F1 was delivered to Ala 14 in March 1999 and deliveries continued at the rate of two per month since. The final updated Mirage F1, was handed over to the Spanish Air Force in April 2001. The new designation was changed into Mirage F1M for the single seaters and Mirage F1BM for the two seat trainers.

Since the Baltic States, Estonia, Latvia and Lithuania are part of the NATO, the air defence of these states is the responsibility of the other NATO members. The mission is called Baltic Air Policing and since March 2004 the alliance nations of NATO have policed the Baltic airspace on a three or four month rotation. On the 1st of August 2006 Spain took over the patrol missions from Turkey. Four Mirage F1Ms trans-

On 19 November 2019, the first regenerated Mirage F1 for US Air Force adversary air training made its first flight. These supersonic radar-equipped aircraft will perform manoeuvres that were not previously possible in adversary air training Draken International's first regenerated Dassault Mirage F1 multirole fighter that will be used in US Air Force (USAF) adversary air training made its first flight in Lakeland, Florida, on 12 November, according to a company statement. The supersonic, radar-equipped Mirage F1 is one of 24 former military fighter aircraft being regenerated by Draken International and assisted by Paramount Group-subsidiary Paramount Aerospace Systems. Sean Gustafson, Draken International vice-president for business development, told the author on 18 November that these regenerated aircraft have been overhauled per technical orders to ensure airworthiness. All systems, the engine, the ejection seat, and more were meticulously checked to ensure a safe aircraft. Along with the acquisition of 24 Mirage F1s and 12 Denel Aviation Cheetah multirole fighters back in 2018, Draken International looks forward to operating all 36 advanced fighter aircraft on Pentagon contracts in 2020. The company was recently awarded a contract as part of the USAF's USD6.4 billion Combat Air Forces (CAF) Adversary Air (ADAIR) programme for combat readiness training. [Draken International]

Details & weapons

ferred to Siauliai Air Base in Lithuania together with more then 80 servicemen. The pilots of Ala 14 scrambled thrice to intercept undisclosed intruders until the mission was taken over by the Belgians on the 1st of December 2006.

On 23 June 2013, the Mirage F1s were officially retired from active service, being relieved by the Eurofighter Typhoon; first to equip was 142 Escuadrón, followed four years later (in 2017) by 141 Escuadrón.

Draken Buys 20 Spanish F1s to Help Train Airmen at Nellis

Draken International on Friday 8 September 2018 closed a deal with the Spanish Air Force, purchasing 20 Mirage F1 fighter aircraft. The supersonic F1s will complement Draken's existing fleet, which is currently flying on contract at Nellis AFB, Nev., supporting the Air Warfare Center. "Our mission is to provide the most cost effective solution to complement organic Red Air assets. We deliver a turnkey solution at a fraction of the cost the Air Force would spend generating the same number of sorties we produce everyday. Not only are we generating four to five sorties for the cost of a single F-16 flight hour, each flying hour preserves valuable life on USAF aircraft. Tremendous savings happen when squadrons are not tapped to go TDY away from their families to support Nellis with an already tiring deployment schedule," said Draken CEO Jared Isaacman. The Mirage F1s are projected to include a helmet mounted cueing system, infrared missile seekers, data link, and electronic jamming from its radar as well as radar warning receiver capabilities.

Details & weapons

Interesting view of a Mirage F1M and its Atar 09K-50 engine. [S.Mafé]

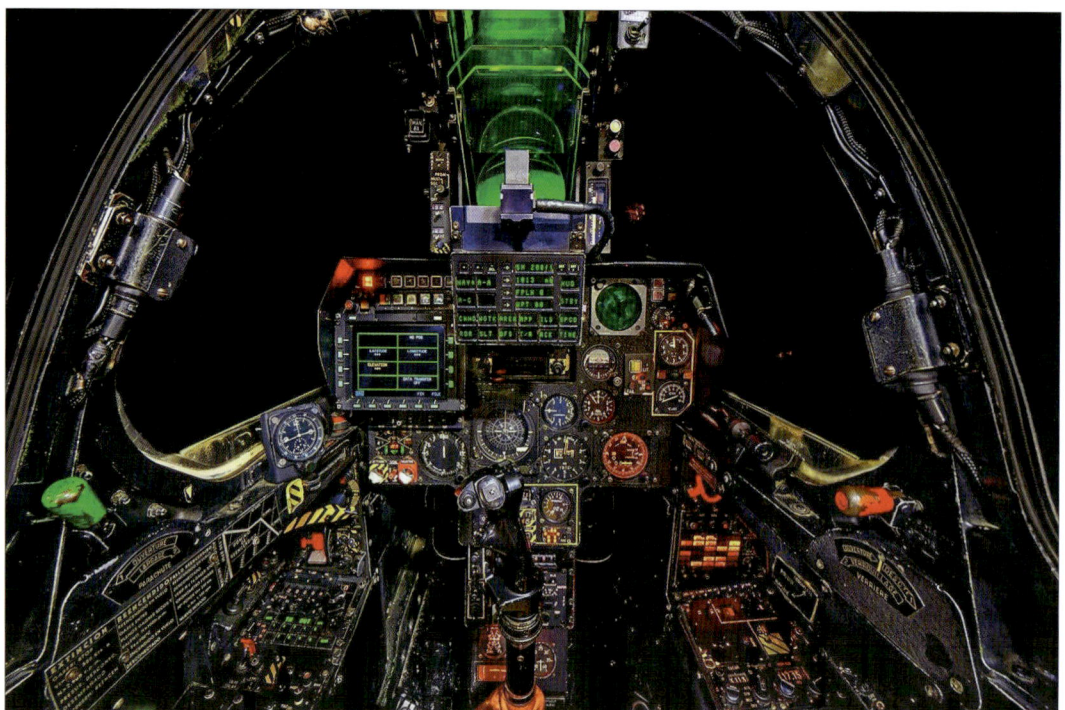

The instrument panel of the F1M showing the digital display indication, the Up Front Panel and the Head-Up-Display. [José Ramos Navarrete]

Details & weapons

Mirage F1M instrument panel showing the modifications which were made. [S. Mafé]

A pair of Mirage F1Ms with inert AIM-9JULI Sidewinders and Barax jamming pods. [Ala 14]

Mirage F1M dropping a parachute retarted bomb (EXPAL BRP250) over the Las Bardenas Reales weapons range in northeast Spain. [Ala 14]

The Cyrano IVM radar as seen in the lectronic shop. [Ala 14]

A brand new Mirge F1EE just after leaving Dassault's factory, still without the squadron insignia and seen at Los Llanos air base, before leaving for its home base, Gando airfield. [S. Mafé]

462 Escuadrón – Ala 46

On April 5, 1999 at 16:00 hours (local), a replacement took place at the 462 Squadron QRA shelter at Gando air base, symbolized by the alert jet.

Captain Cruz in Mirage F1, was replaced by Captain Guerra in F-18A+. It was a solemn occasion and above all, thanks to the professionalism of the members of this unit, there has seldom been such a radical change of material in a squadron being so smoothly and without losing operational capability.

During the years it was equipped with the Mirage F1, 462 Escuadrón "Halcones" (Hawks) made exactly 47,391 flight hours, losing four planes and two pilots (captain Miguel Pérez Moreno in C.14-53 after colliding with Captain Gonzalo O'Kelly Pérez in C. 14-55, who was able to eject, on June 26, 1985, and captain Rafael Sánchez Sánchez in C.14-61 that crashed in the ocean on May 22, 1991.

The Mirage F1 in flight

Gonzalo O'Kelly Pérez, former pilot of Mirage III and F1, tells us in the following lines his

A Mirage F1BE of 462 Escuadrón in its inicial colour schme, later changed to the typical blue of this unit. [S. Mafé]

experience in the EE version of the 462 Squadron:

"The Dassault Mirage F1EE of which 22 units constituted the rooster of 462 Escuadrón of Ala 46, located at Gando air base (Gran Canaria), had some and important improvements with respect to the CE model acquired in 1974 for Ala 14.

The most essential is the ability to refuel in flight using a fixed refuelling probe, located in the nose, in front of the windshield and slightly tilted to the right so that it does not interfere with the pilot's frontal vision when superimposed on his line of sight, with the right side of the windshield.

It also had a really good and extremely useful Thomson inertial navigator in the surroundings of the Canary Islands, where 90% of the flights are made over the ocean, and sometimes very far from the islands.

Finally, the radar was an improved version of the Cyrano IV, with protection against interference, "track while scan" capability, and some possibility of scanning down, if it was not too low.

The rest of the aircraft and its equipment was similar to the CE, as well as the armament capacity and flight characteristics.

The F1 was a considerable advance over the Mirage III, but suffered from the same basic problem: a remarkable aerodynamic profile powered by a mediocre engine in terms of thrust and consumption. If the F1 had mounted the Snecma M53 engine with which it concurred to the socalled "contract of the century" (summoned to replace the F-104 in the air forces of Norway, Holland, Denmark and Belgium, and finally won by the F-16) it would have been a spectacular fighter, but with the Snecma Atar 9K 50 it was just a good plane.

However, what this engine excels in is its reliability and hardness. As a demonstration of what it is capable of enduring, I remember a mission in Las Bardenas weapons range where one of the planes piloted by Captain Mederos swallowed an inadvertent 30 mm projectile which ricocheted and the engine continued to operate for 20 more minutes without the slightest indication of failure, and only started coughing a bit when we were entering traffic pattern in Zaragoza air base, landing without incident. When they took out the engine to examine it, it was discovered that not a single blade of the compressor remained intact, and in some steps there was no trace of up to 50% of them.

It is also a motor that is very resistant to compressor stalls even in very abrupt maneuvers and with a high angle of incidence. And practically immune to the stopages in flight.

It is not necessary to say that the confidence of the pilots in the engine is very great,

and necessary to fly over the sea 600 miles from the base, in a single-engine.

The F1 is a very nice plane for the pilot, without vices, which warns the loss well in advance and always gives it by right, without contrary wink. Only and as in all fighters, some precautions had to be taken when putting g's in the transonic (0.95 to 1.05 Mach).

In the air-ground missions, for which we did not have guided weaponry, it was not a platform as stable as the Phantom, the Mirage III or the F-5, and you had to get the hang of pointing corrections because it was easy to overpower and the smallest error in angle or speed of shot, or if the lever was moved a millimeter when firing, could send the rocket or bomb to another province. Admittedly, although the Phantom pilots could not tell us that they carried as many rockets as us bullets (which was true with the Mirage III), air-ground was not what Dassault engineers had in mind when designing the F1.

The moment of the mid-air collision between the Mirage F1EEs of Gonzalo O'Kelly and Miguel Ángel Pérez on 25 June 1985, the former survided, and later drowned. See the text for details about this incident). [Juanma Vila]

Then Captain Gonzalo O'Kelly Pérez; he retired as a Major and went to fly Spanair Airlines. [via O'Kelly]

A Mirage F1EE after a wheels-up landing at Gando air base, the jet was repaired and continued in service. [Ala 46]

462 Escuadrón – Ala 46

Since its activation as a Mirage F1 unit, 462 Escuadrón owned all the Mirage F1EEs, but a reestructuration of the Spanish AF Mirage F1 in 1992 decreed that all the Mirages belonged to Ala 14, thus its codes changed from 46- to 14- and thus 462 Escuadrón operated both F1CE and F1EE "loaned" from Ala 14. [S. Mafé]

Yet we never looked bad compared to other units.

The F1 is a pure fighter and excelled in aerial combat. Certainly in my time, prior to the arrival of the F-18, it was the best Air Force fighter.

In one-on-one confrontations against the Phantom or Mirage III if the pilots were experts, they could make things very difficult, but in general the advantage was for the F1, especially if the combat was done above 25,000 feet.

If it was the F-5 or the Harrier, the advantage derived from F1's technological superiority was even greater. The radar allowed the F1 could always start the fight in a favorable position and if not, the margins of speed and engine available allowed a "zoom" that left us comfortably 5,000 feet above the opponent. With these two planes, but with the Harrier, it was only essential not to get entangled in a low-speed combat, the classic "dogfight", a situation in which the ability to turn F1 was lower. With speed and height, or changing one by another, it was relatively easy to reach missile firing position, not so much the cannon and is only for a few seconds.

When the F-18 appeared or in the opportunities that the NATO exchanges provided us with fighting with the F-16, the story changed. I still remember the first time I flew a one on one combat with an F-16, and it still stings me. An airplane that holds 9 g's without losing a knot! They will tell me what can be done.

However, if it was two F1 against an F-16, or two against two, and thanks to the great level of training we had in combat tactics in pairs, maintaining mutual support at all times, we achieved very good results. At least one of them we took in the basket.

It is all about getting one of the planes is always pressing one of the adversaries, while the other is repositioned and watches that his partner is not threatened, while giving instructions and informing him of his position and that of the adversaries . When the plane that is "hooked" has difficulty maintaining the pressure without losing its energy, it gives its place to the partner and the papers are exchanged. Said thus seems very simple and in fact this doctrine is invented since the times of Moelders, Galland and Bader, but it is very difficult to implement effectively, and requires much training to maintain an F-16 or an F-18 to defensive all the time, while being denied the support of their own point. This explains the strangeness of a Dutch or Belgian (or Spanish F-18), when we started the post-flight briefing, recognizing the effectiveness of our maneuvers. Or by not recognizing them because you already know, it is very difficult to get a fighter pilot to recognize that they have "put it on" with all of the law, especially if they know that a superior plane is flying.

In short, the F1 was a good plane, in its time a great fighter, which replaced the Mirage III and the Phantom as spearhead of the Ejército del Aire, and suffered the same fate with the arrival of the F-18."

Mid-air collision between two Mirage F1

"On June 25, 1985, in the second flight period of 462 Squadron, a TCA (air-to-air) mission of two aircraft was scheduled. I was the lead of the formation and the wingman was Captain Miguel Angel Pérez Moreno, "Listi" for friends.

In the nomenclature of the TCA era, it means Air Combat Tactics, that is, one-on-one combat, and it involves placing oneself within the parameters of short-range missile or cannon firing. Or said in Christian, to put "a tail" to the other plane.

That day Papayo, which is the radio call sign of the Canary Islands Early Warning and Control Squadron, was out of service due to preventive maintenance. The alternative procedure consisted in proceeding to the D-79 (training area of the Squadron located to the South of the islands), under control of Gran Canaria Approach, to listen to its frequency while we were in the Delta, and return with them to the leave to return to the Base.

The "briefing" included take-off in formation, turn to the assigned course and ascent in tactical formation to the authorized height, and once in the Delta up to 35,000 feet and visual combat. More frequencies to use in each phase of the flight, review the rules of combat, fuel "bingo" and approach and landing procedures. There would only be another formation in the area so we would be in Sector C (in the southwest of Gran Canaria), and they would use sectors A and B that were smaller and located in the Southeast.

The visual combat begins with the two planes flying in parallel, turning 45° outwards and maintaining the course until the separation increases to 4 or 5 miles, at which point the leader orders "turn" and both planes face each other. After that first cross over the two pilots maneuver as best they know until one of them reaches firing position or reaches some of the safety limitations seen in the "briefing": the ground at 10,000 feet, no more than two crosses in scissors, etc.

After completing all the routine procedures prior to the flight, we took off as planned and went to our sector. Once in the Delta we continue climbing to 35 "angels" and just after reaching them we start the separation and seconds later we fly to each other at 2,000 km/h reciprocal speed.

He passes by my left and towards that side we turn both with the afterburner thoroughly. I liked to raise the nose to reduce the turning radius and see the other plane as quickly as possible, but "each master ...". With 90 degrees of turn I see him, and he is doing the opposite, he turns down.

At that moment under the nose and I put g's.

When we cross again I have achieved an advantage of 30-40 degrees, that is to say that we no longer cross front but I am at his ten o'clock and a bit lower. We have lost 3 or 4,000 feet.

When I pass under, I decide to change the turn and try to lose sight of him, since I will no longer be where he will look for me, on his left, but outside his turn, on his right.

Every fighter pilot knows that changing the turn is a heresy unless it is done from a position of certain advantage and you are sure that the other pilot does not see you doing it.

If the maneuver had gone round, at the end of my turn to the right it should have found me between 4 and 6 o'clock in the "Listi" and lower because my longer turn would end with less energy.

During the late 80s and into the 90s the whole Mirage F1 fleet was standardised from the original lizard or blue colour scheme to the Celomer PU-66 NATO light grey scheme, except the nose radome which remained black, until a few years later that these were painted grey also The paint was more resistant against corrosion, a false cockpit was painted underneath the real cockpit. Another change of the Mirage F1 fleet was the assembly of Tracor AN/ALE-40 Chaff/Flare dispensers being located under the horizontal stabilator on both sides of the fuselage, as well as the inddinegounsly developed and buil AN/ALR-300 RWRs. [S. Mafé]

During the years it was equipped with the Mirage F1 (1981-1999), 462 Escuadrón "Halcones" (Hawks) made exactly 47,391 flight hours, losing four planes and two pilots (captain Miguel Pérez Moreno in C.14-53 after colliding with Captain Gonzalo O'Kelly Pérez in C.14-55, who was able to jump, on June 26, 1985, and Captain Rafael Sánchez Sánchez in C.14-61 that crashed in the ocean on May 22, 1991. [S. Mafé]

When I had him back in sight, I was at 6, about 2,000 feet lower and 1 mile. He kept turning left looking for me. I loosened the turn to gain speed and lift my nose towards him. It was almost done.

Immediately I realized that he was turning with very little speed, almost at a stall, because he constantly had to take a turn, even though he was with a low nose.

When I began to lift the nose I noticed that our longitudinal separation had decreased a lot and that I was going to overchute, it was not a very serious problem as far as the result of the combat, all I had to do was let it fall and throw me behind.

But I had it on me, practically it fell on me. At that time and since my ability to maneuver was not much I called on radio "high combat", and without waiting for an answer I pushed the lever to leave quickly from there.

From the beginning of this sequence it was evident that we were going to give a good review, like so many others. All the fighter pilots can count creepy crossings, almost always with airplanes to which it is not seen until they pass you to the side and they put the creeps to you.

The fact of lowering the nose so abruptly saved my life, because tenths of a second later the belly of the "Listi" plane hit the tail of mine.

The plane entered a very violent loss of control, with the nose 60º above the horizon and tremendous vibrations. Control loss procedure: forward lever, centered feet, gases back, works! It seems that I recover it because the plane lowers the nose and stops vibrating.

But before I can breathe I see on my left, outside the cabin, a huge fire. The plane is burning.

Instantly I grab the lower launch command and pull with all my strength, (this command acts half a second faster than the upper one). When the seat acted I lost my vision momentarily because of the approximately 30 g's produced by the explosion in sequence of the three charges that have saved so many lives, thanks to Mr. Martin Baker.

When I regained my sight I was already hanging from the parachute, whose automatic operation has been completed because I jumped below 15,000 feet. I make sure that the dome is correctly deployed looking up, it seems very small.

When looking towards the sea I see my airplane that has split in two, burning and leaving a thick black smoke trail behind.

After the frenzy of the last five minutes silence and tranquility surrounded me, you can only hear the sound of the wind in the strings of the parachute. I try to locate the "Listi" but I do not see him. There is a big boat quite close and I trust you have seen the smoke and the planes falling.

Gradually the adrenaline is decreasing and the relief of being well, joins a feeling of serious responsibility for having lost an airplane that costs several millions.

I go back to the procedures, I check that the emergency equipment hangs from the waistband that identifies those flying French planes, and the folded raft. When I calculate that I am close to the water, I inflate one of the two floats on the waistcoat, a model that has fallen into disuse, fortunately, and that once inflated, two bananas appear under the arms. I also inflate the raft, for which you just have to give a pull to the tape from which everything hangs, and I regret it immediately because the wind makes it oscillate in all directions and comes to hit me a couple of times.

I calculate that the fall lasts about 15 minutes and I prepare to get to the water, only at that moment I was happy not to fall on land because the gale would have left me badly stopped, in fact it was my first parachute jump.

I hit a huge wave with enough force and sank a couple of meters, but I surfaced without difficulty because the wind had dropped the parachute and I had it on. I took off my atalajes, inflated the other half of the vest and got on the raft, where I could only shrink my legs.

After shrinking the water, I opened the survival equipment bags to search for the emergency beacon and connected it. First I checked the operation with negative result, that item did not emit (after the rescue I found out that it did intermittently). I also took out the flare launcher to have it on hand. It had a small bag of water, a can of food, and although the pack of cigarettes had been wet, the rest of the material was in good condition.

The swell was tremendous, and when I did not break a wave on me soaking, I fell off the raft, which I never managed to dry and was as cold as in my life. I opted not to use the raincoat that is equipped with the raft and that only leaves the head, because to fasten it I should have deflated the vest, and with the weight I was carrying I did not want to swim when I pulled again some wave Of course I got dizzy and sunburned myself.

Immediately I thought about my family and it occurred to me that if they rescued me soon I could tell my wife about it, and call my parents, to reduce the fright.

After an hour I started to worry a little, because I was sure that the wind was dragging me a lot, I was afraid of the idea of having it at night.

Another hour passed, and the truth is that my moral was a little on the floor. I was sitting on the raft, legs bent and holding the radio beacon in one hand (apparently still showing no sign of life), and in the other the flare launcher. Suddenly I looked up and a couple of miles away I saw a SAR Super Puma, although it was not flying towards me. I think I broke the world record for the launching of flares, shot the twelve that I had in a heartbeat.

Immediately they saw me and turned to pass over me. It is impossible to express the relief and the joy I felt, I almost fell to the water again by waving my arms with such vehemence.

Then, from the helicopter they threw three smoke markers around me so that the pilot had a more or less fixed reference to fly in stationary, and immediately I had the Super Puma standing on my raft, and the crane began to lower the basket. Previously a rescuer was launched into the water to help me if necessary. When I had her by the side and with the rescuer holding her, I let go of the raft and got inside. I kept the helmet and with the beacon, I was determined to find out if it worked or not, both fell into the water because when I was a couple of meters away from the helicopter, the operator of the crane stopped her to stabilize the basket, and the braking made me release them and grab me to the railings.

The first thing I did after thanking the crew, was to ask for the "Listi" and I was very happy when they told me that they had also located him and that he was very close to there. Then I took off my overalls and they wrapped me in blankets because it was really cold.

One of the pilots came to ask me if I did not care that we were going to pick up the "Listi" instead of going to the Base, because although another helicopter had come out for him, it would take a few minutes to arrive. Naturally I said that I did not care, it is more I would have liked that we arrived together, as we had left.

In a few minutes I noticed that the helicopter stopped, and I peeked into the gate. But we did not see what we all expected.

The parachute floated in the water and there was nothing else, neither raft nor anything. That could only mean that "Listi" was below. It was terrible to witness how the rescuer took him out of the water and put him in the basket with enormous difficulties. But it was even worse when they deposited him by my side in the helicopter, with an hour of flight ahead to reach Gando."

NOTE: The two F1EE Mirage involved were C.14-53 / 462-02 and C.14-55 / 462-04.

111 Escuadrón – Ala 11

The arrival of the first seven Mirage F1EDA/DDAs to Manises-Vañencia air base for service with 111 Escuadrón (call-sign "Dólar"), the flying component of Ala 11, was the culmination of an interesting story which began with the frustrated Mirage IIIEE/DE upgrade – cacelled in July 1991. Once the Spanish Air Staff made the decision to withdraw the Mirage IIIs from service, the only thing that could be done (as nobody wanted to disband Ala 11) was to reequip 111 Escuadrón with a dozen of Mirage F1CE/EEs. This solution was also frustrated, as the maximum strengh the squadron had was eight Mirage F1CEs loaned from Ala 14. In fact this wing, was the owner of the 50 surviving Mirage F1s acquired by Spain 30 F1CEs, 17 F1EEs and three F1BEs), which had to be shared by four squadrons, 111 of Ala 11, 141 and 142 of Ala 14 and 462 of Ala 46. This state of affairs could not last very long and early in 1993 the Ejército del Aire started to look elsewhere for second hand Mirage F1s. After almost a year of evaluating the possible options it was considered that the the best aircraft (in potencial flying hours left, equipment, airframe status, etc) were the eleven F1EDAs and two F1DDAs from the Qatar Emiri Air Force.

All these aircraft had been delivered to the QEAF between March 1983 and July 1984, except serial QA63, delivered in 1992. Its operador was number 7 Air Superiority Squadron (call-sign "Falcon"). Of the original twelve, two of the squadron's Mirages were griten off –QA72 "B" in 1991 and QA62 "T" in 1997 (replaced by QA63). During 1997 this unit received fifteen Mirage 2000-5s, which in turn will be replaced by Eurofighter Typhoons, Boeing F-15QAs and Rafales.

Also evaluated by the Spanish Air Force were the Kuwaiti F1CK-1/2, seven of the former and six of the latter. While there were no two setters available because the the four F1BK-1/2s were taken by the Iraqis and not returned; on the other hand the technical records had been destroyed and its operacional capabilities were not as desirable, while the price asked for them was too high for the available budget. Also visited was Jordan, which offered its 13 surviving F1CJs. Again the price was two high and the offer was turned down. (curiously when these Mirage F1s were phased out of Spanish AF service in 2002, one two seater F1DDA was give to the RJAF!). Finally, eight Iraqi Air Force Mirages embargoed in France were examined, but they were soon discarded as they comprised four two seat F1BQs and six single-seat F1EQ-7, too many of the former and too few of the latter. France offered four F1Cs and one F1B as Exchange for two CASA C-235M transports, and this offer was taken. The five Mirages were delivered to Ala 14 from November 1994, one per month, until March 1995.

Early in 1994 the three sided negotiations started in Earnest –France, Qatar and Spain- for the acquisition of the 13 Mirages. The French parto f the deal was very important, as there was a multmillion dollar contract with the Qataries, not only envolved the Mirage 2000s, a large stock of spares, weapons and training, but also construction of a new air base from the ground up in order that the QEAF should operate for a proper airfield and be freed from the restrictions imponed by operating from a civilian airport as is Doha International. During the negotiation, it was agreed that Dassault would provide technical support for the exQatari F1s delivered to Spain, supplying maintenance services and detaching a technical representative to Manises, Etc. These negotiations continued almost to the eve of the aircraft's departurefor Spain. The price was 17,500 million pesetas (about 1,110.000 € for the 13 aircraft, and advanced flight Simulator, air´to-air missiles, and a complete stock of spares, to be paid during four years of the programme (1994-1997). As

the potencial flight hours of the F1EAD/DDAs, were quited good, and the initial plans were that the Mirage could remain in service untile the year 2010/2013. In QEAF service the had flown relatively few hours, and their average life left since delivery was ten/eleven years, while the last two seater was one of the last F1s built and had only three years of life when the contract was signed.

The contract specified that seven should be delivered during the Summer of 1994, and the remaining six during the second half of 1997. An important stock of spares, the flight Simulator, maintenance equipment and both cautive and 40 operational Matra Super 530F-1 missiles should arrive to Valencia as ship's cargo before the end of 1994, including about half of the seven spare Atar 9K-50 engines.

The Mirage F1EDA/DDA was almost a second generation Mirage F1, the single seat had in fact the pre-installation for adding the air-to-air refuelling probe, including the 8 cm plug venid the radome. The most noticeable thing about htse fighters was their desert camouflage scheme, brown and beige on the upper surfaces and mid-blue on the undersurfaces. These differences were better felt by 111 Escuadrón pilots.

The C.14C/CE.14C (their oficial Ejército del Aire designation), had an integrated nav/attack system, associated to a Dassault Electronique 182 digital mission computer, which received and processed all the information provided by other sensors: Cyrano IV radar (with four air-to-ground modes), Sagem Uliss INS, etc. Mosto f this information was projected in a Thomson-CSF VE-120 HUD, while the armament panel was also different from the Spanish variants, as well as some changes in the cockpit instrumentation, including SEM Martin Baker F10M capable of zero-zero operations.

The first batch was delivered in August 1994, while the second on 28 December 1997. But as Manises air base closed down early the following year, the jets were trasnferred to Ala 14, as well as most pilots and technicians, while Ala 11/111 Escuadrón reformed at Morón air base (Seville), by renumbering Ala 21/211 Escuadrón, initialy equipped with F/A-18A Hornets, and from 2004 to by reequipped with Eurofighter Typhoons.

The F1EDA/DDs continued flying with Ala 14 (142 Escuadrón) until 2002, and the last sortie was in aircraft C.14-82/14-58, on 20 June, flown by Captain Parallé.

Salam malikum manises

Captain Jesús M. García Labajo, who was asigned seven years in the 111 Squadron and therefore piloted the first and second generation Mirage, participated in the two ferry operations from Doha to Manises in 1994 and 1997. This is his personal account of the second, which took place between December 26 and 30, 1997.

"" There are people who choose to travel on Christmas holidays; personally and although it seems a topic, I prefer to spend them with my family. Maybe when we were told that the date for the last Mirage F1 ferry flight from Qatar to Spain would be at that time, we are a little worried if we could take nougat and grapes in Spain or somewhere else in the world. But we got down to work and began to prepare the detachment and especially as we would do the flight from Doha to Manises. Among all those who

Captain Jorge Albalat climbs into the cockpit of a Mirage F1CE loaned by Ala 14 to 111 Escuadrón of Ala 11. [S. Mafé]

A 111 Escuadrón pilot in the "cage" of the F1EDA at Manises air base, November 1996. [S. Mafé]

Salam malikum manises

José Miguel Díaz y Quintana, Mirage III and Mirage F1 pilot, logged about 1300 flight hours in both types with Ala 11 and Ala 14, plus more than one thousand in the C101EB Aviojet casic trainer. Actually he flies the Global Challenger for a corporate company, based in Hong Kong. [Ala 14]

belong to Wing 11 we have done a thorough and meticulous work to prepare the flight and not leave any loose ends. Each had a role and everyone's work should be a good detachment.

Everything consists in coordinating a series of minor works so that the result is the flight of four fighter planes from one base to another separated by 3,500 miles. First you see which path is the shortest, then the most feasible; the best you should propose to the authorities of the country that you are going to fly over to be authorized; you also have to think about minutiae such as where and how you are going to do the technical scales, if you can refuel - do we pay with a credit card or metallic? -, it will be necessary to eat and sleep somewhere; hotels and meals will have to be booked, and you will also have to anticipate how to go from the bases to those hotels. We will need money for hotel expenses, meals, unforeseen events. Well, that's the usual problem. It will be necessary that when we get to take a stopover there are people there to recover the airplanes and repair the small failures that arise, and others must go behind us in case we have to take land in an unforeseen field; We are going to have to ask our Hercules cousins for help, to support us with two planes. How many people do we need? How should we distribute it on each plane? Where will we do the crew relay? If you know how to respond to all that, you already have a lot of cattle. But what worries most is to fly from there to here. Study of the route, fuel consumption, times, speeds, radio frequencies, directions, airfields along the way that can serve you in case there is a problem and you have to take land right away. You have to know how to choose them as they are close to the route, their conditions, services they can provide, if it is a military base or they have already closed it, if it is a civil airport, customs and immigration problems ... Preparing this flight has not been a matter from two or three but from many Manises professionals.

The decision of whether or not to make all the expected jumps would be based on the wind in the face that we knew we were going to find (we expected 100 knots) throughout the route practically. This strong Vienna was going to condition the fuel consumption. Whoever flew the Mirage F1 knows what we are talking about (you can also imagine those who flew the "planchette"). Calculating again and again, we conclude that in the worst circumstances we had sufficient safety margin to reach the furthest alternative. And all the alternatives we contemplated were quite satisfactory to operate from them with Mirage. Prepared the entire flight, we repeat it several times in the simulator. It was within the expected parameters. Of course you have to tell that when you go to the alternative after frustrating the approach, you

Early in 1994 the three sided negotiations started in rarnest –France, Qatar and Spain- for the acquisition of the 13 Mirages. The French parto f the deal was very important, as there was a multmillion dollar contract with the Qataries, not only envolved the Mirage 2000s, a large stock of spares, weapons and training, but also construction of a new air base from the ground up in order that the QEAF should operate for a proper airfield and be freed from the restrictions imponed by operating from a civilian airport as is Doha International. During the negotiation, it was agreed that Dassault would provide technical support for the exQatari F1s delivered to Spain, supplying maintenance services and detaching a technical representative to Manises, etc. [S. Mafé]

Salam malikum manises

know that you will not arrive full of fuel; It is a risk to assume. However, we had room to allow ourselves to make

the decision to start the transfer if that jet did not rise from 120 knots.

Perhaps the most conflicting part of the trip was in the jumps that had to be made from Qatar to Iraklion, in Greece. And I say conflictive because it is not a space in which Spanish fighter pilots have moved frequently. The distances were great and the terrain to fly over unknown: the desert. The doubts that cause the unknown caused us to examine the conditions of each of the alternatives that we could find along the way: we had to foresee everything and leave nothing to chance. In-flight decisions should be the result of prior knowledge of all circumstances.

In the end the decision was to make the ferry in four jumps, making two jumps every day: On December 29, Doha-Tabuk-Iraklion, and on 30 Iraqlion-Solenzara-Manises. On the 29th we were at the base of Doha 45 Spaniards willing to arrive in time to take the grapes in Manises (others in Zaragoza), flying in two Hercules and four Mirage F1.

As planned, at 0230 hours we say goodbye to the staff of the Doha Palace Hotel (very friendly and attentive people, who I think will never be aware of the great service they provided to us and the Air Force); and as planned, the buses that were to transfer us to the base arrived twenty minutes late. However, we had enough time to get to the planes, that the mechanics made them the last minute checks, gather the weather information (everything "seemed" to be fine), coordinate last details, put on the flight equipment and get on the planes. Everything was ready to return to Manises with the four Mirage. All the hours of preparation and study of the routes we were going to follow, the telephone conversations held, the numerous messages sent and received, the essays made in the simulator, all the effort and work of those who were in Doha and of those who they had stayed in Manises was going to be tested now.

AME3147, the first Hercules, would take off at 04.00, while the F1 would do so at 05.00, bound for Tabuk, in Saudi Arabia. We had planned the flight in two couples: AME1117 with two fighters and AME1116 with a fighter and a two-seater. 1117 took off from Doha at 05.10, and 1116 at 05;20. Later the second Hercules did it (AME3146). We were following the shortest route between Doha and Tabuk (about 900 miles). We said before the weather situation "seemed" to be fine: it was as planned. Right on the nose we had the 100 knot wind jet (about 180 knots) that we expected. That wind was going to stop us from flying faster and therefore it would take longer; the distance that could have been covered in an hour and a half was going to be almost half an hour more. Half an hour to spend a fuel, which in a fighter plane never exceeds. Although we knew that we were within the calculated margins, it is not funny about flying over the desert and seeing how the fuel distiller runs.

"Doha, AME1117, Salam Malikum, request start-up clearance". With this radio communica-

The Mirage F1EDA/DDA was almost a second generation Mirage F1, the single seat had in fact the pre-installation for adding the air-to-air refuelling probe, including the 8 cm plug venid the radome. The most noticeable thing about htse fighters was their desert camouflage scheme, brown and beige on the upper surfaces and mid-blue on the undersurfaces. [S. Mafé]

Salam malikum manises

The C.14C/CE.14C (their oficial Ejército del Aire designation), had an integrated nav/attack system, associated to a Dassault Electronique 182 digital mission computer, which received and processed all the information provided by other sensors: Cyrano IV radar (with four air-to-ground modes), Sagem Uliss INS, etc. Most of this information was projected in a Thomson-CSF VE-120 HUD, while the armament panel was also different from the Spanish variants, as well as some changes in the cockpit instrumentation, including SEM Martin Baker F10M capable of zero-zero operations. [S. Mafé]

tion, the 1117 leader began the ferry mission to bring the F1EDA / DDA from Doha to Manises. The four took off and proceeded without news. Everything was going as planned. The tension of being concentrated in what you were doing almost didn't let you admire an incredible landscape: the desert. Part was hidden by a sea of low clouds that covered almost the entire Arabian Peninsula. But when that sea dissipated, if you could contemplate that overwhelming view. The desert was everywhere. It was lost on the horizon, and from the narrow cabin of the Mirage F1 you could almost feel like Saint Exupery on its Courrier du Sud flight over the Sahara. Sometimes the desert looks wrinkled and mountainous, like the skin of a melon, others are reddish, and sometimes simply light brown, clear and extensive, as far as you can see. Sometimes you discover down there a tiny greenish dark spot: an oysis. You can also distinguish the hand of man over nature. There are some towns and small villages near those dark spots and some lines that come from the horizon and go to where you can't see: they are a network of roads built by the Arabs (or their petrodollars) that cross the desert from east to west and from North to south. What is not seen are service stations. Almost an hour had passed, and we were seeing all this desert when, almost asking for forgiveness, the controller warns us of something that dislodges our plans: Tabuk, our destiny is closed; There are sandstorms. You have to decide and fast. The alternatives we had planned are in conditions of reduced visibility, and if we take before Tabuk, we can not then make the flight to the next planned stopover, Iraklion; We should do another one before. The controller informs us of the weather in Wejh.

It is on our list; It is further, but of course it is the one that offers better weather conditions. It seems incredible that this happens to us; We completely ignore the desert: here it is also bad weather, apart from the sun in summer. Also with just fuel. We must decide and quickly: .... Wejh is the one that is farther away, but it is the one that is better, and it will also allow us to take the next jump to Crete, we will arrive with little fuel, but we arrived, it was something we knew that It could happen and we secured our margin. The leader of AME1117 communicates to Jeddah Control our decision: we go to Wejh, 10,000 feet of track. When we got up that night, who was going to tell us that we were going to know this track.

We already knew about memory the approach to Tabuk maneuver, but we have changed our destination, and we must change the date. At that moment, the amplitude of the cockpit of a commercial plane is missing, with two pilots, space to deploy letters, draw manual approximations, etc ... In the cockpit of an F1 you have the right place, and you are alone . You can only carry the right cards and you can't wait to need them to stop to look at them. You must have studied all the approach maneuvers before getting on; It is not the time to study them, if not, who will fly the plane? Looking at the pen, you find the ILS RWY 31 approach letter to OEWJ: this is the correct one. Taking advantage of free seconds, you review what you already know: approach course, heights, speeds, frequencies, minimums. And by the way a new calculation of fuel: this time of two hours of flight, they will be almost twenty minutes more. Twenty minutes of continuing to spend fuel; Luckily we had left a margin of fuel for this.

Salam malikum manises

After two hours of flight we begin to descend for the approach. Jeddah Control knows that we carry the right fuel, and it shows you worried about giving us priority. In those moments it is when you must have cold blood and show yourself that you are worth what you are doing. However, you also have a warm heart. Fifteen miles away the track is already distinguished, long, there is also a very long white beach, with pale blue sea, coral reefs, where sharks hide, and at the end of the track, about two kilometers away A small population With the field in sight, Jeddah transfers us frequently from Wejh. Surprise!, there are no controllers, the frequency is for coordination with other airplanes. Fortunately, the only one that responds is an Arabian Airlines plane, which tells us that it waits for us to take land to take off it. We are really all very close to the shot.

In tactical frequency, we notify AME3146 of our position. If there is no problem you will not need to come here, the next communication would not be until two hours later. For them a good time of uncertainty begins and we know that they will be worried about us: will everything go well ?, we hope so.

AME1117 enters first and warns that everything is clear. When the 1116B takes the one of Arabia Airlines takes off (a 757 seemed to me). And we started rolling towards the platform. You see a terminal building in the background, small but relatively modern. And there is also another commercial parked with people going up, a small fire station and a fuel tanker. As we get closer we discover that our signalists are going to be the members of a police force that are beginning to appear. Before stopping the engine, we enter the data for the next flight into the navigation system; the commercial leaves, and the only thing you see is the police in front of the plane. Whether you like it or not, you start to worry. A lot of armed policemen in front, a previously unauthorized route and an airport where they would have no idea that four fighter planes from a foreign country from another country with which they do not have very good relations to say were going to land. Of course, that no war machine is more harmless than a fighter in the parking lot, without armament of any kind and with 800 liters of fuel (the most).

With all the cabin work finished, stop the engine. There is the serious problem of getting out of the cabin without a ladder or anything while two Arab policemen are watching you. When I "fall" to the ground I don't know if I can take out my passport or wait for them to see no suspicious movement in me, when they square and square a military salute of the most martial, pure English style. "Salam Malikim," and that begins with Arab hospitality. The "director" of the airport comes to appear: he is a lieutenant of the Royal Air Force of Saudi Arabia. It falls apart in compliments and bein-

A two-seater Mirage F1DDA seen at Manises flight line during its ferry flight to Los Llanos-Albacete air base, once this air base closed down. [S. Mafé]

Due to a higher than expected attrition rate, the Ejército del Aire sought more airframes in the early 90s. Part of the solution came from Qatar since their Mirage F1s were in surplus as they favoured the new Mirage 2000-5. The first ex-Qatari Mirage F1 arrived in Spain on 23 Augusts 1994. In total, eleven single seaters (Mirage F1EDA) and two two seaters (Mirage F1DDA) were delivered to Spain until the year of 1997. Meanwhile used six-eight Mirage F1CEs loaned from Ala 14. [S. Mafé]

venidas and tells us that everything is already organized, that we go to rest. While the most modern (someone had to touch …) they stay to refuel the airplanes, the rest we go to the VIP room, where the servants offer us coffee (Arabic) and tea, dates, sweets, water, etc. … An excellent rest and a good relax. The lieutenant, to whom we are infinitely grateful for his hospitality, offered to help us with everything we needed, while giving orders to attend us. All the time we stayed in Wejh was to refuel, since the tank had little capacity and had to get more fuel before starting with the second plane. We would have liked to spend more time in Wejh, to have taken a bath in those crystalline waters (they insisted that without sharks), to have known that small town on the west coast of Arabia, with a friendly people but could not. But it was December 29 and we had to get to Manises, and we had many miles to go. As we disconnected the hose from the tank of the last plane, we got on as we could to the planes and started the second jump: Wejh-Iraklion, where we would sleep. We sincerely thanked the lieutenant for his hospitality and the support provided, which we did not count on when they told us about the situation in Tabuk.

It is curious to start, roll and take off without requesting authorization from anyone, just notify Jeddah Control that you have already taken off and that you proceed according to the route. Once heading 317 degrees to Egypt, we left behind 140 minutes of exciting flight, in which we had to demonstrate how it flew while maintaining optimal conditions, flying over a unique landscape and moments of firm and safe decisions, in front of us It was not only to arrive in Manises, but the satisfaction of having done it as planned and getting the Air Force to have a total of 12 Mirage F1 more, with increased capabilities thanks to its integrated navigation and armament system, which They give more precision and autonomy, as well as Matra Super 530F1 medium range missiles. The initial destination of the aircraft is Manises. Later, possibly Albacete, but those who brought them from Qatar were the "maniseros".

The truth is that along the way we have only found hospitality and kindness, and we can say that the preparation, planning and study of everything we could foresee has borne fruit: on December 30 we arrived in Manises with the four Mirage F1EDA / DDA and two Hercules. And with all the staff on board. The Ala 11 has since then and until the moment of its deactivation with 12 F1 quite different from its cousins of Albacete and the Canary Islands, with navigation and armament systems that ensure their superiority in attack and defense missions.

The 11th Wing has successfully carried out the transfer of airplanes, weapons and material from Doha to Manises with success (thanks to the help of the C-130 of Zaragoza, which without them we would not have been able to do). An unforgettable experience and the feeling of having done a good job among all. The F1 are in Manises.

Beginning of a new time

Many thanks to the staff of Doha, Wejh, Iraklion, Solenzara: "Sucran, mahsala, Merci, Au revoir."

Jorge Albalat Estela

111 Escuadrón pilot, nine years at Manises air base

When I arrived at Manises Air Base in June 1990, I never imagined the adventures and misadventures that awaited me.

And a few months ago, convalescent of a disease, came to my hands a copy of the Aeronautics and Astronautics Magazine, whose "dossier" spoke of the modernization of Mirage IIIE. I do not know if because of the illness or the illusion of the project, my initial idea of requesting destination to the F-18 was transformed into requesting a vacancy in my hometown and that of my family, Valencia, flying the plane that I had always dreamed of since small: the "plancheta". And above modernized! Since I was very young I looked out the window of the school, with the consequent punishment, when in the morning they flew over it.

The modernization project looked good, and overflowed with enthusiasm. But during the first weeks of work in Manises things were no longer what they seemed. Problems began to arise in the definition of the project, both cell and avionics and its integration through software. What if you finned canard yes, canard no, development of software similar to that of the F-18, etc. So in the late 90's there was talk that the first prototype would not be available until in about 5 years!

The unit, to all this, continued to receive new pilots for the future ground attack squad. But as time went by the problems grew and new obstacles arose. The situation did not look good. To make matters worse, the national economy was not going through good times, much less defense budgets. And what was already feared ended up happening: the project was suspended in the spring of 91. Everything remained in the air: our future, the Base, the airplanes, etc. And now that?

Beginning of a new time

Again we went back to the streets. Because not long ago, Wing 11 would be dissolved and the "planchets" removed, transferring the C-101 of 41 Group to Manises. At the last moment everything was changed, considering the modernization of Mirage III. Well, nothing, everything fell apart again and we were back to the beginning.

Bulos, dimes, diretes, I have heard, I have been told, it may be that they bring the F1 of the Canary Islands, that they buy F-16 that the Americans have left over, buy more F-18, close the Base ... of everything.

The answer came in autumn of 91. At that time the Unit had about 8 captains (of the 3 that were when I arrived destined in June of 90). We met the pilots in the briefing room and a new directive issued by JEMA was read. It was amazing! A squadron was created in Manises that was to be integrated into the NATO Immediate Reaction forces, endowed with 12 Mirage F1. Were we dreaming? It was truly a professional challenge, and demanded an important process of transformation. But then the inevitable questions arose: Where were they going to get 12 F1? Who was going to give us the instruction? How was the Base to be restructured? And above all, what was it and what should a NATO

> These negotiations continued almost to the eve of the aircraft's departure for Spain. The price was 17,500 million pesetas (about 1,110.000 € for the 13 aircraft, and advanced flight Simulator, air-to-air missiles, and a complete stock of spares, to be paid during four years of the programme (1994-1997). As the potencial flight hours of the F1EAD/DDAs, were quite good, and the initial plans were that the Mirage could remain in service until the year 2010/2013. [S. Mafé]

Beginning of a new time

In QEAF service they had flown relatively few hours, and their average life left since delivery was ten/eleven years, while the last two seater was one of the last F1s built and had only three years of life when the contract was signed. [S. Mafé]

immediate reaction squad do? Where was the regulations? Was it really possible to have a squadron of those characteristics operational or was it just a house of cards, a utopia?

The Directive contemplated a fact that would later also be decisive in this whole situation, and it was that all Mirage F1 became "administered" by Wing 14 in relation to maintenance and assignment of them to each user unit, including those of Canary Islands. This allowed the F1EE that until now only flew in the Canary Islands, were flown by Albacete and Manises, beginning to practice refueling in flight.

The instruction of the 111 Squadron pilots would be carried out by the 142 "Tiger" Squadron, which assumed the work of the F1 Conversion Unit (School). The staff of pilots would be nourished by those already belonging to 111 plus a group of pilots from the 462 Squadron of the Canary Islands, most of whom were still in training. The instruction process would be carried out in two batches, given the availability of the 142 Squadron. Thus, the first round formed by two Manises pilots plus the "canaries" began

(and in other cases continued) the instructional phase in Albacete in January 1992. The course was adapted to the experience of each one (3 levels), and it would last until September 30 of that year. On that date, the "planchetas" on Wing 11 would be dropped, replacing the first six F1, and in turn the second batch of pilots, all of Manises, would be incorporated to receive instruction in Albacete. In June of that year, the 80,000 flight hours of the Mirage III, a penultimate tribute and pre-departure to the unit's flagship aircraft for more than 20 years, would still be celebrated.

And it arrived on October 1, 1992, for which a nice day was organized both for the farewell of the "planchetas" and for the reception of the F1, including military act, glass of wine, dinner and even a failure with a "planchette" of cardboard. There was also an air parade of all the fighters of the Air Force units, and many pedestrians and "iron workers" of all life attended, giving with their presence a warm farewell tribute to Mirage III.

From that same day on October 1, the first batch of pilots began operating from Manises with the six F1s mentioned, and the second batch of pilots, all from 111 Squadron, who had been flying the Mirage III until then, were they incorporated the 142 Squadron to receive their instruction, and thus complete the template of the future IRF squad.

Thus, in the fall of 92, we started operating from Manises with limited capacity, all this motivated by the limited combat qualification that almost all pilots had except those more veteran on the plane. We were in the spotlight of many controls and units, and we had to start slowly and safely. Safety first! More than an annoyance

Rafael Núñez, a veteran Mirage III and F1 pilot with Ala 11 and Ala 14. [Ala 14]

it cost the squad leader to stop the feet of a pilot who intended to step on the gas. At six months we were getting combat aptitude, beginning to participate in exercises in early 93, especially in DAPEX air defense, with great enthusiasm and desire to do well, aware that, as mentioned above, there were many watchful looks.

But during those months a series of events were going to happen that were going to completely change the future of the squad. Since on the one hand the F1 logistics chain was going through a very hard time due to budget cuts. And on the other hand, Wing 14 had a series of unfortunate accidents during 92, in which the loss of two magnificent people and pilots had to be regretted. All this had a very negative influence on the operation of the fleet, and little by little the survival of the new squad was becoming increasingly difficult. So that both Albacete and the Canary Islands would be seriously affected in their operation. Such situation began to be very worrying for the command, so the entire initial project of the 111 IRF Squadron collapsed with a new directive issued by the General Staff of the Air Force. And although the existence of the 111 Squadron in Manises was maintained, the aircraft were reduced to nine (instead of 12), and would no longer be part of NATO's rapid reaction forces. At least they didn't close the Base and dissolve the Unit, which was the fear of all the components. But of course, we would no longer have priority in terms of operating aircraft, spare parts, electronic warfare equipment, etc. All this in practice relegated us to the background And thanks!

At the end of the spring of 93 the second batch of pilots was incorporated that was under instruction in Albacete, some problems arising. On the one hand the few assigned flight hours had to be distributed among more pilots. On the other hand some of the newcomers were older but with lower operational qualification than pilots of the first round. But well, everything was overcome. And in September 1993, the first squad exchange took place with the 334 Squadron of Iraklion, based on the island of Crete (Greece). It was an unforgettable experience. They also began to participate in real weapon shooting exercises, which was a challenge for novice pilots, since it was the first time that real bombs were thrown at a firing range in front of many commanders.

The Unit continued its pace of work like any other Unit of the Air Force, except that we were not alarming, due to the low number of aircraft and pilots. Although yes, the Unit proposed the command to enter alarm on successive occasions. But luckily or unfortunately, the service was never assigned.

Meanwhile the bulos continued their course. The Air Force had created a commission to study the purchase of more F1. It was commented that they had been in France, in Kuwait, in Qatar, etc. "Hey, they've told me ... that if the Qatar models have" mission computer "... Will the F1 they buy be for the 111 Squad?" We all thought that of course it was the right thing, of course! Months went by, we read the commission's reports, how good the Qatari models looked! It was like a dream coming to Valencia. And the dream came true. In the spring of 1994 the JEMA issued a directive providing the 111 squadron of 13 Mirage F1EDA / DDA aircraft, with simulator and armament included. However, not everything was really positive, since they were to be purchased in two phases, so that seven planes would come in the summer of 1994 and the rest in December 1997. Three years later! The simulator and part of the armament would come in the first round. But electronic warfare did not enter into the contract. Anyway, it wasn't going to be all perfect. And there was little money.

The first phase "Qatari" Mirage F1s arrive to Manises

At the beginning of summer we received the order to prepare the expedition to Qatar to bring five planes, since the other two had to be picked up in France. During the trip we would be supported by two C-130H Hercules, as well as Dassault and Snecma staff. They sent us a manual of the plane in perfect French, and based on photocopies we began to study the plane a bit. The jumps of the Doha-Valencia trip were organized, always thinking of going on fuel surpluses when arriving at the successive airports, unknown to us. Overflight authorizations, entry visas were requested in some countries, flight plans, get letters and cards of the aerodromes of scale, alternative and emergency,

Captain Francisco "Paco" Almenta, a 111 Escuadrón walks to his jet for a DACM mission. [S. Mafé]

The first phase "Qatari" Mirage F1s arrive to Manises

These differences were better felt by 111 Escuadrón pilots. The first batch was delivered in August 1994, while the second on 28 December 1997. But as Manises air base closed down early the following year, the jets were trasnferred to Ala 14, as well as most pilots and technicians, while Ala 11/111 Escuadrón reformed at Morón air base (Seville), by renumbering Ala 21/211 Escuadrón, initialy equipped with F/A-18A Hornets, and from 2004 to by reequipped with Eurofighter Typhoons. [S. Mafé]

talk to embassies, and endless tasks with very little timeframe. To all this the dates were a little in the air, with which all the work we carried with pins. Finally we embarked in August 1994 on a Hercules heading to Qatar to bring the planes to Spain. A month before the maintenance team had already moved to prepare the planes and learn as much as possible from them. After two days of flight we reach the hell of August in Doha: 50 degrees and 80% humidity. Can you fly like this? we were wondering.

After two weeks of stay, a few small courses on the plane, simulator sessions, double-flying flights with the French instructor, loose on the hunt, and above all, once the financial problems between the two countries have been solved, we take our way to Spain with four fighters and a double control, escorted by two C-130H Hercules. The journey was made in two days, following the Doha-Yeddah-Cairo-Tanagra-Solenzara-Valencia route. We arrived in Valencia on a hot August day, which for us was not hot at all, of course.

Having already own aircraft in the Unit, the "La Mancha" models we had were reduced to four, so that the pilots were divided into two groups, each group flying a single model of aircraft: "Qatari or Manchego". And of course, sometimes some flew more and others flew less. The Qatari model could be installed the Manchego engine with slight modifications, but not the other way around. And we began to experiment and learn to operate the Qatari on our own, studying first in the manuals and then putting it into practice, because nobody knew anything at all. First bombing missions at the Bardenas weapons range, missions with the Matra Super 530 captive missile, handling of the inertial for attack missions, having the Maintenance squadron used to it. It was not easy to operate two different models at the same time, both for maintenance and operational reasons, especially if we had to fly in formation. In any case, we continued with our usual activities of maneuvers, detachments, air-to-air shooting, squadron exchanges, etc; In short, normal activities. To all this, as we had a long time to go until 1997, we tried through reports and studies to improve the operational capabilities of the Qatari F1s, aware that there was little money for improvement programs, and that there were other priorities.

However, from 94 to 97 the squadron, despite the limitations of the material reached a good operational and tactical level, as we demonstrate in important maneuvers alongside other NATO units, such as the "Central Enterprise" exercise carried out in Germany for two weeks.

At the same time, the Base was preparing to operate with the 13 aircraft: armament workshops, test benches, electronics workshop, etc.

A new building was built to house the simulator, installing successfully and becoming fully operational. Everything was going at a good pace. One day they told us that the unit's endowment would no longer be 13 aircraft, but 12, since one of the F1 had just crashed in Qatar during an exhibition flight, its pilot being unharmed.

And so the months went by, writing many reports and proposals that would improve the operation of the plane: refueling in flight, software, new radios, and other series of equipment and systems.

Second and final phase of a great unit

And finally it was time to pick up the rest of the remaining planes in Qatar, as well as to end the endless logistical trips of Hercules tirelessly managed by the equipment of the material area, parts cataloging, workshop preparation, maintenance, etc. Since these areas are the most voluminous and sacrificed at the time of carrying out a Unit, having spent entire months in Qatar dedicated to these purposes.

The first step was to receive the aircraft, moving three tester pilots to receive the aircraft. As they were Christmas dates and Ramadan was approaching, this group returned along with the rest of the staff before Christmas Eve, and after Christmas Day the second group of pilots would be transferred to bring the planes to Spain in 4 jumps. This time 1 jump was eliminated, making the route: Doha-Arabia-Crete-Corsica-Valencia. But when the team of testers and material returned to Valencia on December 19, 1997 to spend Christmas, the reception could not be worse: We closed the Base!

But if we have not yet brought the airplanes, nor finished the maintenance work-

The author (left) with Captain Jorge Albalat after a flight in an 111 Escuadrón Mirage F1DDA in February 1996. [Javier Valero]

The F1EDA/DDs continued flying with Ala 14 (142 Escuadrón) until 2002, and the last sortie was in aircraft C.14-82/14-58, on 20 June, flown by Captain Parallé. [S. Mafé]

Second and final phase of a great unit

By the summer of 2002 all the Mirage F1EDA/DDAs were withdrawn from service in Ala 14, in spite of having flight potencial for about two more years, but they were not compatible with the upgraded Mirage F1Ms. One F1DDA was provided to the Royal Jordanian Air Force. [S. Mafé]

shops, nor installed the test benches! And what will happen in the future? Our families, our houses, ...

It was a very sad Christmas for all Base staff. Even so, the planes of Qatar were brought with the professionalism characteristic of the people of Manises, not without the occasional aventurilla typical of these "Ferry" flights, aware of the uncertainty of the future.

Once the drink was digested, we were still hoping that someone would come out in our defense, that it would have been a rash decision, seen everything that happened to the Unit in recent years, that the weight of history would weigh on the command. During the first months of 1998 we did not stop speculating about the future, clinging to any data that allowed a slight hope. But in the early spring of '98, during the first important meeting on the closure of the Base that took place in Manises, the clear and concise command of the command was transmitted: the airplanes should be at the base of Albacete on October 1 of that same year, that is, in six months. The matter was very serious, and there would be no going back until July 1999.

The last months that preceded the transfer of the airplanes to Albacete ran with a certain "normality", as if nothing happened. But in reality the Base was closing. All the personnel were pending of their new destinies, the material was being distributed to other bases, the spare parts of F1 to Albacete, closing of workshops ...; in short, everything followed its process. For their part, the pilots also had their "diaspora", being assigned to the General Academy of Air, Torrejón, Canarias and the largest group that

Second and final phase of a great unit

A three view of Mirage F1EDA C.14C-76/11-03, seen at Albacete Air Depot after maintenance, it could be clearly seen the Qatari camouflage scheme, as well as Ala 11 badge. [Tono Fernández Leonarte]

was destined just before the transfer to Wing 14, along with their planes.

And it arrived on September 29, almost six years after that October 1, 1992, when the F1 arrived in Manises, the planes were ready to leave. After a simple act of farewell, and the presence of representatives of Dassault and Snecma, the Qatari F1 under the Colonel C.O. of Ala 11 took off towards Albacete, where they were received with another simple act. They were already part of Ala14. More than one pilot of the 111 Squadron who participated in the transfer later acknowledged that at the time of starting his pulse trembled, a lump in his throat was made and his eyes shone. But the last mission of the 111 Squadron had to be accomplished, and so it was.

Pilots and airplanes would still be seen by the Base for a few months, either because the simulator was still operational, or because revisions to the airplanes continued.

Only the process of deactivating and closing the Base was pending.

Although in practice there was no longer a squadron or Ala, the official deactivation of both was formalized along with the closure of the Manises Air Base in July 1999 ...

The Mirage F1 F1EDA/DDA early phase out

In spite of having still enough potential for flight hours in the cells and systems of the ten Mirage F1EDA and two F1DDA (known as the "Qatari"), on April 30, 2002 a message from the General Staff was received in Los Llanos del Aire for a meeting in Madrid that would take place two weeks later. The issue to be addressed was Milestone No. 8 (Intent to disenroll from C14C / CE.14C).

After this meeting, on June 7, 2002, the Material Section of the Logistics Division of the EMA issued a document signed by the JEMA, which stated the following:

– Taking into account logistic conditions related to capacity of maintenance of Wing 14 and the number of flight hours required to the Unit for the year 2002, the total number of available aircraft results high. That is why airplanes that remain idle are waiting for shift for revisions or repairs when they are not necessary to maintain the operability requested to the Unit.

– The decommissioning of the "C" model will allow pilots to fly all their hours on the same model, thus increasing their operability and safety, by not having to fly two different models.

– In addition it would allow to concentrate all the maintenance personnel of Wing 14 in work on a single model, with the advantages of training and preparation. The replacement quantity of the C14M would be increased, with the use of common C.14C equipment as a replacement.

The aforementioned document also outlined that the check-out process should take place immediately for all aircraft except C.14-77 and C.14-80, which would take place no later than June 4 (interestingly, the document is later than this date) and August 30, 2002 respectively. On the other hand, the material that has been decommissioned - all airplanes - is kept in the Wing 14 empty of fuel and without any explosive or flammable material. The common elements with the C.14M will be used as a replacement for it. In addition, the

The exercise comprised sea, air and land operations and demonstrates NATO's resolve and capability to maintain stability in the Balkans. It is directed by the Commander of KFOR and coordinated by the Joint Force Commander within the NATO HQ responsible for the Balkans Operations (CINSOUTH). Both are under the supervision of the Supreme Allied Commander Europe (SACEUR). [Ala 14]

possibility of INDRA using the simulator parts of C.14C (stored in Albacete since its transfer from Manises in 1999) to that of C.14M is being studied.

A roof is also under construction in which to store the aircraft cells (fuselages without planes, without hydraulics, fuel, explosives, etc.). Attempts to sell them to another Air Force (Argentina, Ecuador, Morocco) were unsuccessful, and in the latter case, recently for obvious reasons. Perhaps it would be time to reserve one of them for a monument at the Los Llanos Air Base, or perhaps two, one with the colors of Wing 14 and another with those of Wing 11, to remember his career in the Air Force. Thus, since the arrival of the first seven in Manises in August 1994, the Mirage F1EDA / DDA made a total of 7,422.25 flight hours.

Rapid Guardian 2003

From 15 January to 15 February 2004, Reserve forces put into practice a new operational concept that enabled them to deploy more rapidly and deal with any military contingency in Kosovo and the region.

The Operational Rehearsal, Rapid Guardian 2003 (RG 03) took place in Kosovo and involved a newly organised pool of forces committed by NATO and Partnership for Peace countries. These forces, which comprised Operational Reserve Forces (ORF) and Strategic Reserve Forces (SRF), are dedicated to the Balkans.

RG 03 was one of a continuing series of training events to ensure that units assigned to the SRF and other Reserve Forces designated for operations in Kosovo and Bosnia and Herzegovina, were ready for action at any time in the KFOR area of responsibility. KFOR is also participating in the exercise to demonstrate its commitment and improve its ability to conduct cross-sector combined operations.

The exercise comprised sea, air and land operations and demonstrates NATO's resolve and capability to maintain stability in the Balkans. It is directed by the Commander of KFOR and coordinated by the Joint Force Commander within the NATO HQ responsible for the Balkans Operations (CINSOUTH). Both are under the supervision of the Supreme Allied Commander Europe (SACEUR).

U.S. Armor troops based in Germany and Marines from the United States have left Kosovo after their success in the month-long operational rehearsal Rapid Guardian 02-3. The event demonstrated KFOR's resolve to deter illegal smuggling and border crossings, and its ability to reinforce with units from both inside and outside Kosovo.

Rapid Guardian 02-3 was a very successful operation that increased stability along Kosovo's border with the Former Yugoslav Republic of Macedonia. [Ala 14]

Rapid Guardian 2003

After the end of Operation Allied Force in June 1999 and the deployment of a NATO-led land force, called KFOR (Kosovo Force), the situation began to calm down, so that the air forces of countries began to withdraw gradually of the Atlantic Alliance involved in these missions. [Ala 14]

On Friday, January 10, Wing 14, with three Mirage F1M, C.14-66 / 14-38, C.14-70 / 14-42 and C.14-73 / 14-45, 38 people, including six pilots, two intelligence officers, a noncommissioned officer of Electronic Warfare, a crypto-custodian and 28 of the always effective and vital maintenance members and gunsmiths, supported by a C-130H of Wing 31, left for the air base of Gioia del Colle, in southern Italy. [Ala 14]

Soldiers of Task Force 1-35 Armor, part of the U.S. 1st Armor Division based in Germany, and elements of the 25th Marine Regiment, based in the United States, worked as part of KFOR MNB (E) in the last phase of the event, which began July 11 with an airborne insertion by soldiers of the U.S. 173rd Airborne Brigade, based in Italy, and which included augmentation by a United Kingdom company from MNB (C) and a German company from MNB (S).

MNB (E) also provided its Brigade Reconnaissance Troop to MNB (S) during the event.

Rapid Guardian 02-3 was a very successful operation that increased stability along Kosovo's border with the Former Yugoslav Republic of Macedonia.

Facts about Rapid Guardian

An airborne task force of 173 soldiers from 1st Battalion, 501st Parachute Infantry Regiment, part of the U.S. Army's Southern European Task Force in Vicenza, Italy, conducted a drop into the MNB (E) area of responsibility on July 11. Once on the ground, the soldiers participated in training and peacekeeping patrols with KFOR units for approximately two weeks.

As the SETAF soldiers were about to redeploy, a second iteration of approximately 100 soldiers from 1st Battalion, 35th Armor Regiment, part of the U.S. Army V Corps' 1st Armor Division, arrived along with some 200 U.S. Marines from Company G, 2nd Battalion, 25th Ma-

Rapid Guardian 2003

The missions themselves began on Monday, January 13 and lasted until Friday 17. On the same Friday after completing the last two missions they made return flight to Los Llanos. [Ala 14]

A total of twelve sorties were made in Rapid Guardian, it must be added the six sorties made between the deployment and return. The average of the departures was 4:30 hours per mission, although the days that were not supported by the tanker plane (KC-135R of the USAF or C-135FR of the French Armée de l'Air based in Istres) the time was It reduced to about 2:45 hours. This happened on one occasion, when the tankers could not take off from the base near Marseille, due to the accumulation of ice and snow on the track and adverse weather conditions. [Ala 14]

rine Regiment, based in the United States, to conduct similar operations.

U.S. Air Force transport aircraft from the 86th Airlift Wing in Germany supported the deployments of personnel from Europe.

Approximately 100 soldiers from the U.S. Army V Corps' 1st Infantry Division in Germany have deployed as a supporting element with six AH-64 Apache attack helicopters and crews. The Apaches self-deployed to Kosovo over a four-day period and were integrated into operations on the ground in Kosovo during the initial part of the rehearsal.

One German company of about 70 soldiers and one United Kingdom company of about 120 soldiers also participated in ground operations.

The rehearsal provided an opportunity to practice the U.S. European Command's capa-

Rapid Guardian 2003

For the Ala 14 pilots, the missions consisted of collaborations in air-ground operations, either interdiction of the battlefield (BAI) or air support (CAS) practicing guiding and simulated bombing by the ground controllers of the various forces, both of IFOR (Bosnia), and KFOR (Kosovo), always under the control of "Magic", the E-3 Sentry on duty at that time, which could be British, French or NATO. They also launched BE11C/A practice bombs on the Resolute Barbara Range (located north of the city of Glamoc in Bosnia and Herzegovina). [Ala 14]

bilities to quickly deploy forces into the region. The assets involved represent additional U.S. resources for NATO's use in maintaining a secure environment in the Balkans.

Ala 14 supports Multinational forces in the Balkans

After the end of Operation Allied Force in June 1999 and the deployment of a NATO-led land force, called KFOR (Kosovo Force), the situation began to calm down, so that the air forces of countries began to withdraw gradually of the Atlantic Alliance involved in these missions. Thus in 2000, the British closed their detachment in Gioia del Colle, in December the Canadians said goodbye to Aviano, later they would be followed by Turks and French; the Americans of the 31st Fighter Wing - increasingly committed to the detachments to Turkey and Kuwait, to control the exclusion zones in northern and southern Iraq - participated less in surveillance operations. Finally, the Air Force decided that it was also time to close its famous Icarus Detachment of the northern Italian air base of Aviano, which took place in July 2002 (although a KC-130H and four

F-18A+ remained "on call "in Spain in case its presence was necessary.

From that situation, the planners of NATO's Fifth Allied Air Force, whose area of responsibility covers Italy and the Balkans, devised a type of exercise to maintain the physical, continuous and rotating presence of NATO aircraft over the Balkans - mainly Italians, French, British, North American and Spanish - to show the flag and exercise with the allied forces deployed in Bosnia-Herzegovia and Kosovo. In this context, after Christmas, it was the turn of Ala 14 (its first contact with the Balkan theater of operations). On Friday, January 10, Ala 14, with three Mirage F1M, C.14-66 / 14-38, C.14-70 / 14-42 and C.14-73 / 14-45, 38 people, including six pilots, two intelligence officers, a noncommissioned officer of Electronic Warfare, a crypto-custodian and 28 of the always effective and vital maintenance members and armourers, supported by a C-130H of Ala 31, left for the air base of Gioia del Colle, in southern Italy.

The missions themselves began on Monday, January 13 and lasted until Friday 17. On the same Friday after completing the last two missions they made the return flightto Los Llanos air base.

A total of twelve sorties were made in Rapid Guardian, to which must added the six sorties made between the deployment and redeployment. The average of the sorties was 4:30 hours per mission, although the days that were not supported by a tanker (KC-135R of the USAF or C-135FR of the French Armée de l'Air based in Istres) the flight time was reduced to about 2:45 hours. This happened on one occasion, when the tankers could not take off from the French airfield near Marseille (Istres), due to the accumulation of ice and snow on the runway and adverse weather conditions.

Rapid Guardian 2003

For Ala 14 pilots, the missions consisted of collaborations in air-ground operations, either interdiction of the battlefield (BAI) or air support (CAS) practicing guiding and simulated bombing by the ground controllers of the various forces, both of IFOR (Bosnia), and KFOR (Kosovo), always under the control of "Magic", the E-3 Sentry on duty at that time, which could be British, French or NATO. They also dropped BE11C/A practice bombs on the Resolute Barbara Range (located north of the city of Glamoc in Bosnia and Herzegovina).

This detachment demonstrated, as the important deployment to Eielson AFB, Alaska, had done before, the new capabilities of the F1M, which with its excellent avionics that exceeds in some respects that of the F-18, can go and operate where Hornet goes, being single engine, is not an obstacle to perform these operations. But to understand this revolution that took place in Ala14, as a step prior to the arrival of Typhoon ten years later, we should review what was the Mirage F1 Modernized. A few months later, Wing 14, specifically the 142 Squadron (the first deployment was made by 141 Squadron pilots), returned to participate in Rapid Guardian.

F1M of Upgraded

The modernization program of the C.14 was awarded to the company Thomson (currently Thales), which in turn made a series of subcontracts with companies of very diverse nature, from ATE in South Africa for software development, EADS CASA for the serial production of aircraft, etc …

But these processes are not easy, and Ala 14 suffered, waiting to have its entire fleet delivered and operational, many months of low availability of F1, airplanes that were constantly delivered for modernization, losing part of the operation which for many years these and other pilots managed to achieve.

By then (2003) the C.14M was already a mature product, two years ago the last of the aircraft was incorporated into the Unit.

Currently, the new possibilities of the plane allow to carry out the mission entrusted with much greater reliability and safety. Reliability for the accuracy of the information provided by the new equipment; security by having the pilot much more time to monitor the outer space, space where you usually have to do the work. And all this because, once again, it is necessary to insist that the best preparation of the mission on land will offer greater possibilities of success in flight. This is one of the main features of the new technology: to be able to plan the mission in great detail and with many different options. covering not only the initial plan, but also possible modifications already in flight.

The pilot's main tool in preparing his flight is the Mission Planning System (SIPMA) of the Air Force or the MIS (Mission Interface Station). In the different work stations available, the pilot will prepare his mission, later entering all the data in the PDS (Portable Data Store). And from there to the plane. But let's analyze a little more in depth how this planning is done, especially in a ground attack mission, which is the main role of Wing 14.

Naturally, the first thing that the pilot must know is what his objective is, not only physical, but also the damage that must be caused, if applicable. And starting from the existing Battle Order, the route had to be chosen to follow and get to the target. Therefore, it must take into account existing land threats, entry and exit

> This detachment demonstrated, as the important deployment to Eielson AFB, Alaska, had done before, the new capabilities of the C.14M, which with its excellent avionics that exceeds in some respects that of the F-18, can go and operate where Hornet goes, being single engine, is not an obstacle to perform these operations. But to understand this revolution that has taken place in Ala14, as a step prior to the arrival of Typhoon ten years later, we should review what is Mirage F1 Modernized. [Ala 14]

Rapid Guardian 2003

A few months later, Ala 14, specifically the 142 Squadron (the first deployment was made by 141 Squadron pilots), returned to participate in Rapid Guardian. [Ala 14]

The first upgraded Mirage F1 was delivered to Ala 14 in March 1999 and deliveries continued at the rate of two per month since. The final updated Mirage F1, was handed over to the Spanish Air Force in April 2001. The new designation was changed into Mirage F1M for the single seaters and Mirage F1BM for the two seat trainers. [Ala 14]

corridors, expected weather conditions, masking with the ground and other endless details that would be too broad to list. The first result of this entire study is the selection of six types of possible attacks on the assigned target (of which its position is naturally known), each of which may be clearly different from the previous one. Thus, in what is called Program Attack, the pilot can choose between the following shooting modes: - AUTO - CCIP - LOFT - CANNON.

In AUTO or CCRP (Continuous Calculation of Release Point) mode, the pilot designates the target and subsequently authorizes the shot. From that moment on, you can start the escape maneuver, releasing the system previously preselected armament on the ground when the algorithms introduced consider it convenient. In the CCIP (Continuous Calculation of Impact Point) mode, you can visualize in the HUD where your weaponry will fall when you release it. If you have chosen to perform a LOFT, a certain ascent will start from a certain distance from the target, and, once the shot is authorized, the armament will perform the parabola necessary to reach it, allowing the aircraft to remain outside the coverage of the enemy defenses. And all this by previously selecting the safety height from which the pilot should not descend, the sensors that he will use for greater accuracy, the number of pumps he will use on each occasion, and the trail or space that they should occupy in If more than one are the ones that are going to be launched.

Therefore it can be said that the ability to program six different types of attacks offers a wide range of possibilities. But there may always be opportunity targets, and here we find the Quick Air to Ground function, where, without knowing the situation of the target beforehand, the pilot can choose between six other possibilities, selected as before the shooting conditions. To get to the objective it is necessary to avoid enemy defenses, and for this there is an editable database by the pilot in which they will introduce their situation, including their lethal area as well as the necessary codes for a correct interpretation of the weapons system to which each r threat. And avoiding those areas, the successive "waypoints" or turning points will be chosen. The F1M does not have its own designation capacity for laser-guided bombs ("auto designate") thus it had to depend on an FAC or an F-18.

Rapid Guardian 2003

Advanced Systems

Taking a leap forward, it is worth commenting that when flying your route, the pilot can choose between two types of navigation: Tactics Gímanse and Rote Gímanse. Clarified these concepts, and returning to the mission programming, the pilot had to correctly choose the distances chosen for each waypoint as Present Route and as Future Route. Subsequently, already in flight, the pilot will choose at any time which type of navigation is more suited to the need of the moment. If he choose the second one, it can select between PR or FR. These possibilities, apparently complex, give a great versatility to the pilot's performance.

Each timepoint can be associated with one hour of overflight, so that by choosing the "Speed Guidance" function, the speed at which the pilot must fly will be displayed in the HUD, also indicating by means of a graphic symbol whether to increase its speed, keep it or reduce it. But are all the waypoints the same? Absolutely. Some will be defined as turning points, others as targets, others as an airstrip (which will allow an inertial approach to be made so that the aircraft is in the Final Approach Fixed perfectly aligned with the runway and at the height that it has finally entered). Other types of "waypoints" include "Emergency", which will remain operational even if the Mission Computer fails.

The preparation does not end here. It remains to define the actual configuration of the aircraft, as well as the simulated for better training. And up to five different flight plans can also be introduced, each clearly different from the previous one if necessary. All this set of information introduced in a commercial computer is converted into a file, which the pilot can transfer to the PDS (Portable Data Store-Data Transfer Module) before finally going to the plane.

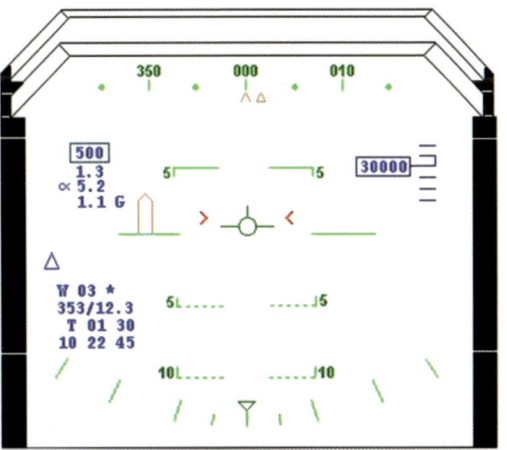

The HUD in tactical mode. [Ala 14]

During the late 80s and into the 90s the whole Mirage F1 fleet was standardised from the original lizard or blue color scheme to the Celomer PU-66 NATO light grey scheme., except the nose radome which remained black, until a few years later that these were painted grey also The paint was more resistant against corrosion, a false cockpit was painted underneath the real cockpit. [Rafael Treviño]

The Up Front Control Panel showing a waypoint. [Ala 14]

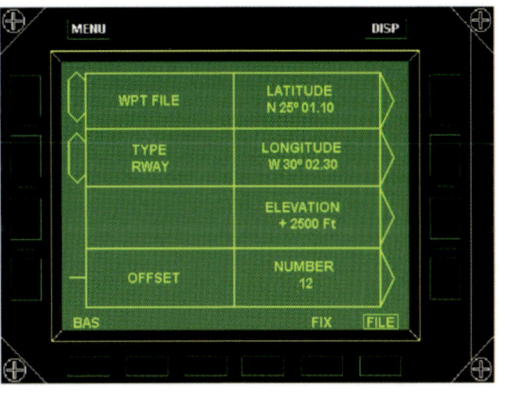

Data presentation in the multifunction display. [Ala 14]

Harrier AV-8S/TAV-8S & AV-8B/B+/TAV-8B

Rapid Guardian 2003

Another change of the Mirage F1 fleet was the installation of Tracor AN/ALE-40 Chaff/Flare dispensers being located under the horizontal stabilator on both sides of the fuselage. The Air-to-Air missiles were upgraded from AIM-9N Sidewinders into AIM-9JULI, which included a seeker unit of the AIM-9L to give improved capabilities. Until the arrival of the EF-18 Hornet, the Mirage F1 was Spain's top fighter. [S. Mafé]

Rapid Guardian 2003

Once the specifications of the programme were set, the modernisation contract, valued at US$96m, was awarded to Thomson-CSF RCM (now Thales Group) in October 1996. It covered a Service-Life Extension Programme (SLEP) and an avionics upgrade for 48 F1CE/EE single seaters and four F1EB (CE.14) two-seat trainers. Spanish companies like Amper Programas, Indra and CASA (the later then part of part of EADS) acted as sub-contractors, together with ATE of South Africa. The latter was responsible for the design and integration of the navigation, display and weapons systems. [S. Mafé]

Mirage F1M inside one of 22 Hardened Aircraft Shelters (HAS) at Los Llanos-Albacete air base. [S. Mafé]

The two seat Miragre F1BM underwent a rather basic upgrade, including the AN/ALR-300 radar warning receiver. [S. Mafé]

Major Diego Sánchez Caamaño, C.O. of 142 Escuadrón during 2007-2009, a highly experienced Mirage F1 pilot, with almost 3.000 hours logged in the jet. [Ala 14]

Colonel Miguel Moreno Álvarez was in command of Ala 14 from August 2002, until August 2004. In his credit he has more than 3,200 flight hours (+2,800 in fighter jets), the majority at the controls of Mirage III, since he was posted three times in Ala 11 of Valencia. He was replaced by Colonel Felix Sahagun Shwartz, also an old "planchetero". [S. Mafé]

This PDS has small dimensions, approximately those of a pack of tobacco, so it is very convenient to use and transport.

And the time has come to go to the plane. The PDS and the videotape are now attached to the traditional flight equipment, which, due to its excellent characteristics, allows the pilot's front view or the multifunction display (MFD, Multifunction) to be recorded with a very good color quality Display- Multifunction Screen). The duration of the tape allows, except for very long flights, to record the entire mission, which means a great advantage when all communications and flight incidents are recorded. If necessary, you can select a function that will automatically record certain moments of the flight.

Naturally, the first action to be carried out will be the alignment of the navigation system, consisting of a GPS enslaved to an inertial platform. This set allows different navigation modes, with commendable accuracy. At the same time, all the data recorded in the PDS will be transferred to the Mission Computer, although it should be noted that, if necessary, any of them could be edited and modified, using both the UFCP (Upper Front Control Panel- Post of Viewfinder Command) as the MFD.

At any time during the mission, the status of all new systems can be checked through the visualization in the MFD, and the indication that appears in the HUD is available as an alert. Therefore, before take-off, the pilot knows the state of the systems perfectly.

During the flight there are four specific programs associated with the new functionalities:

NAV Navigation
A-A: Air-to-Air
PRG: Air-to-Ground programmed
A-G: Air-to-Ground of opportunity

A tiger stripped Mirage F1M belonging to 142 Escuadrón. [S. Mafé]

Each of them will have a different representation and input of data both in the HUD and in the MFD, being able to eliminate the pilot certain data when he considers that they are not necessary.

On the same screen, the pilot can select a representation of his position with respect to any of the flight plans that the system has previously memorized, using the previously mentioned functions of Tactical Guidance or Route Guidance.

During the flight the pilot will change mode, as seen above, often using the buttons located on both the joystick and the gas lever, bringing the design closer to the HOTAS concept. But not only the pilot selects the most convenient mode in each case, but you can also use the most important functionalities of each in the same way, that is, without having to release the hands of both levers. This again allows a greater concentration on what is happening in outer space, earning a few tenths of a second that can be vital.

The upgraded Mirage F1M in a close-up view

The Mirage F1M instrument panel. [JM Sales]

A 141 Escuadrón pilot climbs into the F1M cockpit. [JM Sales]

The upgraded Mirage F1M in a close-up view

The Ejército del Aire was the second air force to order the Mirage F1. Due to its central position in the mainland of Spain, a new wing of the then Air Defence Command was commissioned on Base Aerea Los Llanos-Albacete to be equipped with the new Mirage F1 fighter.

The new wing; Ala 14, or more precisely 141 Escuadrón (squadron), received the first machine directly from Mont-de-Marsan in France and handed over on 18 June 1975. Soon after, the first squadron of Ala 14 was equipped with 16 Mirage F1CEs and became fully operational.

The upgraded Mirage F1M in a close-up view

Apart from the SLEP, the upgrade package included a revised cockpit configuration with a multi purpose colour liquid crystal display and a Smart HUD from Sextant Avionique, now part of Thales as well. Another novelty was the Sextant Inertial Navigation System with GPS interface, NATO-compatible Have Quick 2 secure communications, Mode 4 digital IFF, a defensive aids suite, including the AN/ALR-400 radar warning receiver, and flight recorders. The cockpit lighting became compatible for night vision goggles and hands on throttle and stick (HOTAS) and some enhancements to the Cyrano IVM radar for accurate ground-attack and mapping capabilities in four different modes was implemented. The upgraded prototype of the Mirage was prepared by SABCA in Belgium and made its debut flight in April 1998. The remaining aircraft were modernised in Spain by CASA (now Airbus Defence & Space) at Getafe (Madrid). The first upgraded Mirage F1 was delivered to Ala 14 in March 1999 and deliveries continued at the rate of two per month since. The final updated Mirage F1, was handed over to the Spanish Air Force in April 2001. The new designation was changed into Mirage F1M for the single seaters and Mirage F1BM for the two seat trainers. [S. Mafé]

The upgraded Mirage F1M in a close-up view

Mirage F1M "14-21" outside its HAS on a rainy day, note the practice bomb dispenser fitted on the centerline station. [S. Mafé]

The upgraded Mirage F1M in a close-up view

A pair of Mirage F1Ms inside the QRA shelter, December 2011. [S. Mafé]

Unfortunately the first one crashed on 4 January 1977. A further batch of aircraft equipped the already newly formed 142 Escuadrón from April 1980, and in October that same year the first two seater (Mirage F1BE) arrived. This wing focused their training on interception tasks and in January 1982 they reached the milestone of twenty five thousand flight hours. Not uncommon these days, the whole wing operated from flight lines in the open air but this changed when the first hardened shelters were built to accomodate the Mirage F1s in 1985. The multirole Mirage F1EEs were delivered from October 1981 until March 1983 and transferred to 462 Escuadrón as part of Ala 46 based at Gando-Las Palmas Air Bawe, in the Canary.

The Spanish Mirage F1s were delivered from 1975 through 1983, with the machines obtained in three separate batches. In total 45 F1CEs, 22 F1EEs multi-role and 6 F1BE two-seaters were delivered. In the beginning, the F1CEs and F1EEs were designated C.14 and the F1BEs CE.14. The F1CEs and F1BEs were originally delivered with sand/brown/green camouflage topside and light gray underneath, while the F1EEs were delivered with medium blue on top and light gray on the bottom. The F1BEs assigned to Ala 14 received the same camouflage as the F1CEs.

Due to a higher than expected attrition rate, the Ejército del Aire sought more airframes in the early 90s. Part of the solution came from Qatar since their Mirage F1s were in surplus as they favoured the new Mirage 2000-5. The first ex-Qatari Mirage F1 arrived in Spain on 23 Augusts 1994. In total, eleven single seaters (Mirage F1EDA) and two two seaters (Mirage F1DDA) were delivered to Spain until the year of 1997. The Spanish realised that the airframes were in perfect condition and hence

The upgraded Mirage F1M in a close-up view

The HGU-55/P helmet belonging to then Lieutenant Fernando Caballero de Pro, posted to 142 Escuadrón. [S. Mafé]

During the late 80s and into the 90s the whole Mirage F1 fleet was standardised from the original lizard or blue colour scheme to the Celomer PU-66 NATO light grey scheme., except the nose radome which remained black, until a few years later that these were painted grey also. [S. Mafé]

the Spanish put them in service immediately. They continued to maintain their two-tone brown and blue colour scheme. All Mirage F1EDAs and Mirage F1DDAs became operational in 111 Escuadrón of Ala 11 at Manises-Valencia Air Base, replacing the loaned Mirage F1s of Ala 14. The same deal included additional engines, spare parts and 40 Matra Super 530 radar guided AAMs. More airframes came from the Armée de l'Air. One surplus two-seater and four single seaters delivered between November 1994 and March 1995 became part of Ala 14 and retained their medium blue camouflage until the midlife modernisation programme. But the life of the Mirage F1 at Ala 11 was limited. Manises-Valencia AB was to be closed due to budget cuts and relocation of assets so all the Mirage F1EDAs and DDAs were moved to Ala 14 by the end of September 1998. In total Spain received 91 Mirage F1 of four variants, and in the post F-86F Sabre, it was the second biggest fast jet fleet, only surpassed by the EF-18A/B, F/A-18A fleet, with 96 examples and closely followed by the C101EB Aviojet basic trainer with 88 examples.

Upgrading the fleet

During the late 80s and into the 90s the whole Mirage F1 fleet was standardised from the original lizard or blue color scheme to the Celomer PU-66 NATO light grey scheme., except the nose radome which remained black, until a few years later that these were painted grey also The paint was more resistant against corrosion, a false cockpit was painted underneath the real cockpit. Another change of the Mirage F1 fleet was the assembly of Tracor AN/ALE-40

The upgraded Mirage F1M in a close-up view

Ex – Qatari Mirage F1EDA seen at an Ala 14 maintenance hangar after being withdrawn from service in 2002. [S. Mafé]

Chaff/Flare dispensers being located under the horizontal stabilator on both sides of the fuselage. The Air-to-Air missiles were upgraded from AIM-9N Sidewinders into AIM-9JULI, which included a seeker unit of the AIM-9L to give improved capabilities.

Until the arrival of the EF-18 Hornet, the Mirage F1 was Spain's top fighter. After the introduction of the Hornet in 1986 the Mirage F1 still remained an important asset for air defence and ground attack. An avionics and service-life upgrading programme was investigated in the beginning of the 90s. Once the specifications of the programme were set, the modernisation contract, valued at US$96m, was awarded to Thomson-CSF RCM (now Thales Group) in October 1996. It covered a Service-Life Extension Programme (SLEP) and an avionics upgrade for 48 F1CE/EE single seaters and four F1EB (CE.14) two-seat trainers.

The upgraded Mirage F1M in a close-up view

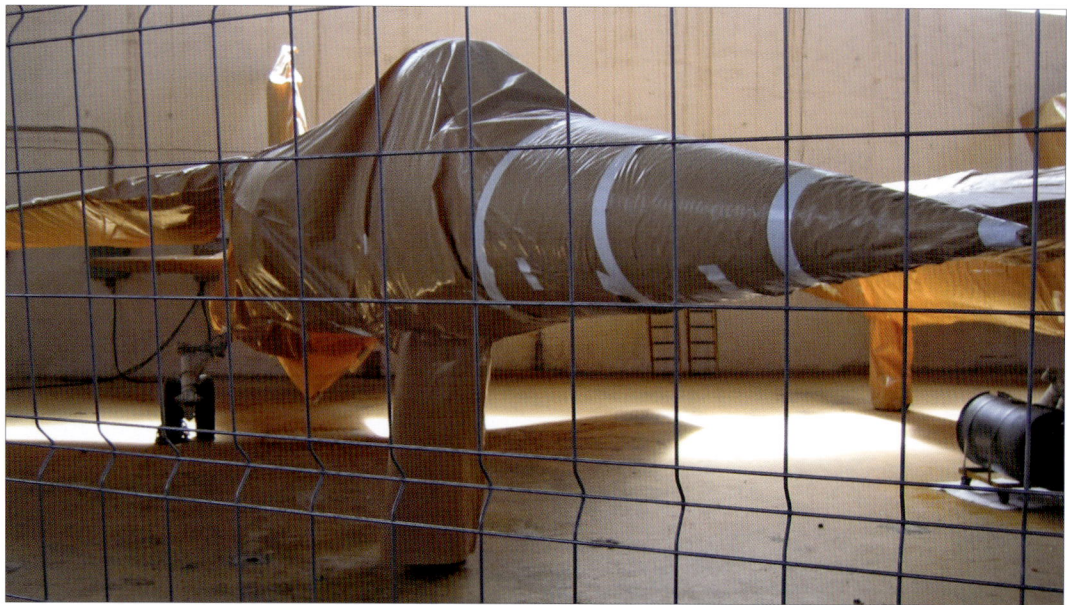

During the early 2000s a few Mirage F1Ms were preserved, as there were more jets than pilots, and returned into service in 2006/2007. [S. Mafé]

The upgraded Mirage F1M in a close-up view

Two Mirage F1s are gate guards in the plaza near Ala 14 command building, the first serailled "14-01", is a former Qatari F1EDA. [S. Mafé]

Spanish companies like Amper Programas, Indra and CASA (the later then part of part of EADS) acted as sub-contractors, together with ATE of South Africa. The latter was responsible for the design and integration of the navigation, display and weapons systems.

Apart from the SLEP, the upgrade package included a revised cockpit configuration with a multi purpose colour liquid crystal display and a Smart HUD from Sextant Avionique, now part of Thales as well. Another novelty was the Sextant Inertial Navigation System with GPS interface, NATO-compatible Have Quick 2 secure communications, Mode 4 digital IFF, a defensive aids suite, including the AN/ALR-300 radar warning receiver, and flight recorders. The cockpit lighting became compatible for night vision goggles and hands on throttle and stick (HOTAS) and some enhancements to the Cyrano IVM radar for accurate ground-attack and mapping capabilities in four different modes was implemented. The upgraded prototype of the Mirage was prepared by SABCA in Belgium and made its debut flight in April 1998. The remaining aircraft were modernised in Spain by CASA (now Airbus Defence & Space) at Getafe (Madrid). The first upgraded Mirage F1 was delivered to Ala 14 in March 1999 and deliveries continued at the rate of two per month since. The final updated Mirage F1, was handed over to the Spanish Air Force in April 2001. The new designation was changed into Mirage F1M for the single seaters and Mirage F1BM for the two seat trainers.

Figure 1

In Tactical Guidance, the system informs the course and distance pilot directly to the next "waypoint" or turning point, regardless of their current position.

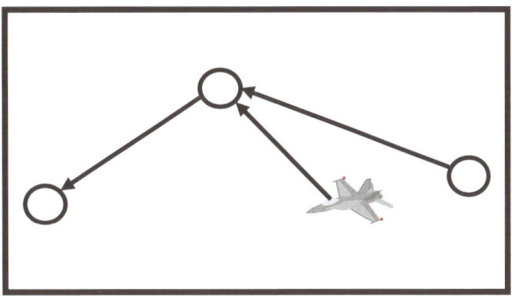

Figure 2

In Route Guidance, the pilot can choose between arriving at the next "waypoint" with a certain advance (which he will define) according to the initial route ("Present Route"), or making sure that before flying over the next "waypoint" he will find himself already with the following course, establishing in advance what the anticipation ("Future Route") is.

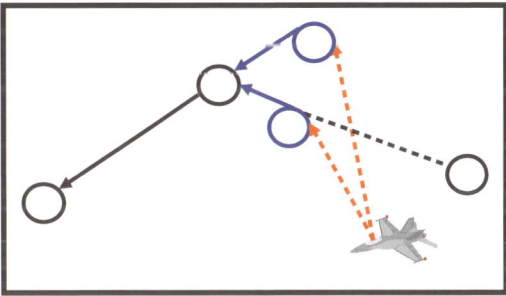

Clarified these concepts, and returning to the mission programing, the pilot must correctly choose the distances for each "waypoint" as "Present Route" and as "Future Route". Subsequently, already in flight, the pilot will choose at any time which type of navigation is more

The upgraded Mirage F1M in a close-up view

The second "14-91", is one of the four ex Armée de l´Air F1Cs purchased second hand, these were not upgraded, and only received the AN/ALR-300 radar warning receiver. [S. Mafé]

The Mirage F1M had a good electronic capability as seen in this photo with a Syrel ELINT pod in the centerline, and a Barax jamming pod in the right outboard wing station. [Ala 14]

suited to the need of the moment. If you choose the second one, you can select between PR or FR. These possibilities, apparently complex, give a great versatility to the pilot's performance.

Each timepoint can be associated with one hour of overflight, so that by choosing the "Speed Guidance" function, the speed at which the pilot must fly will be displayed in the HUD, also indicating by means of a graphic symbol whether to increase its speed , keep it or reduce it. But are all the waypoints the same? Absolutely. Some will be defined as turning points, others as targets, others as an airstrip (which will allow an inertial approach to be made so that the aircraft is in the Final Approach Fixed perfectly aligned with the runway and at the height that it has finally entered). Other types of "waypoints" include "Emergency", which will remain operational even if the Mission Computer fails.

The preparation does not end here. It remains to define the actual configuration of the aircraft, as well as the simulated for better training. And up to five different flight plans can also be introduced, each clearly different from the previous one if necessary. All this set of information introduced in a commercial computer is converted into a file, which the pilot can transfer to the PDS (Portable Data Store-Data Transfer Module) before finally going to the plane. This PDS has small dimensions, approximately those of a pack of tobacco, so it is very convenient to use and transport.

And the time has come to go to the plane. The PDS and the videotape are now attached to the traditional flight equipment, which, due to its excellent characteristics, allows the pilot's front view or the multifunction display (MFD, Multifunction) to be recorded with a very good color quality Display- Multifunction Screen). The duration of the tape allows, except for very long flights, to record the entire mission, which means a great advantage when all communications and flight incidents are recorded. If necessary, you can select a function that will automatically record certain moments of the flight.

Naturally, the first action to be carried out will be the alignment of the navigation system, consisting of a GPS enslaved to an inertial platform. This set allows different navigation modes, with commendable accuracy. At the same time, all the data recorded in the PDS will be transferred to the Mission Computer, although it should be noted that, if necessary, any of them could be edited and modified, using both the UFCP (Upper Front Control Panel- Post of Viewfinder Command) as the MFD.

Accidents and incidents of the Mirage F1 (C.14) in the Air Force

- 30.03.76 C.14-1 / 141-01 (Dassault Mirage F1CE) (see 10.05.83 / 30.05.05), Ala 14 (BA de Albacete), aborts a takeoff in its BA, being stopped by the braking barrier.
- 04.01.77 C.14-2 / 141-02 (Dassault Mirage F1CE), Ala 14 (BA de Albacete), crashes in Lezuza (Albacete), in approximation to his BA, his pilot, Captain Marco Antonio García Gea, dies.
- 07.04.81 CE.14-26 / 141-23 (Dassault Mirage F1BE), Ala 14 (BA de Albacete), crashes in Villa de Ves (Albacete), due to problems with the flight controls, Captains José Antonio Company Follana and Fidel Galán Benavides, eject safely.
- 10.03.82 C.14-17 / 141-17 (Dassault Mirage F1CE), Ala 14 (BA de Albacete), the train is folded during landing on its BA, although the plane was later recovered; the pilot, Lieutenant Manuel Fernández-Roca Teigell was unharmed (see 13.06.89 / 15.10.90).
- 28.09.82 C.14-46 / 142-41 (Dassault Mirage F1CE), Ala 14 (BA de Albacete), crashes in Alhama de Granada (Granada), due to a collision with a bird, during a low-level mission, its pilot, Captain Joaquín Sánchez Díaz ejects, resulting in less serious injury.
- 10.05.83 C.14-1 / 141-01 (Dassault Mirage F1CE) (see 30.03.76 / 30.05.05),Ala 14 (BA from Albacete), the train is folded during landing on its BA; without consequences for the pilot, captain Pedro Enrique Díaz Iglesias; The plane was later recovered.
- 11.10.83 C.14-12 / 141-12 (Dassault Mirage F1CE), Ala 14 (BA de Albacete), crashes in waters in front of Motril (Granada), having been able to eject from it Captain Pedro Vera Estela.
- 14.12.83 First Corporal (AAR) Gabriel Huertas Ramos dies when the ejection sequence of the seat of C.14-54 / 462-03 (Dassault Mirage F1EE), of 462 Escuadrón, Ala 46 (BA de Gando, Gran Canaria), while performing maintenance work on it.
- 01.06.84 C.14-65 / 462-14 (Dassault Mirage F1EE), of 462 Escuadrón, Ala 46 (BA de Gando, Gran Canaria), is struck of charge after catching fire during a refueling in BA de Gando (Gran Canaria).
- 14.09.84 C.14-5 / 141-05 (Dassault Mirage F1CE), Ala 14 (BA de Albacete), crashes in Casas de Haro (Cuenca), during a TCA (Air Combat Tactics) mission, causing the death of Captain Salvador Ramírez Montoro.
- 27.02.85 C.14-35 / 142-30 (Dassault Mirage F1CE), Ala 14 (BA de Albacete), crashes in Villasequilla de Yepes (Toledo), when it collides with a high-voltage tower, of Captain José Luis Valdés Ayesta, killed. The plane took part in a DAGA exercise.
- 25.06.85 C.14-53 / 462-02 (Dassault Mirage F1EE) and C.14-55 / 462-04 (Dassault Mirage F1EE), both of the 462 Escuadrón, Ala 46 (BA de Gando, Gran Canaria), collide in flight over the Atlantic Ocean about 40 miles southeast of the Island of Gran Canaria, both pilotsejecting, although Captain Miguel Ángel Pérez Moreno (aboard the first plane) died, Captain Gonzalo O'Kelly Pérez of the second being rescued alive, during a mission in air combat training. Captain Pérez Moreno died drowned as a result of losing consciousness during the ejection, hitting his head during it.
- 29.01.86 C.14-25 / 142-26 (Dassault Mirage F1CE), Ala 1414 (BA de Albacete), crashes in El Ballestero (Albacete), during the approach phase to its BA, 141 Escuadrón commanding officer Francisco Serrano Lázaro killed.
- 24.09.86 C.14-58 / 462-07 (Dassault Mirage F1EE), of 462 Escuadrón, Ala 46 (BA de Gando, Gran Canaria), is damaged in the Leeuwarden AB (Netherlands), during an exchange of NATO squadrons, when the landing gear is inadvertently retracted; The plane was repaired. Without consequences for Captain Gabriel Baquero Dancausa.
- 02.12.87 C.14-18 / 14-18 (Dassault Mirage F1CE), Ala14 (BA de Albacete), during the landing at this airfield, the train folds, suffering minor damage, being unharmed its pilot, Captain José Valdecabrera Llorens.
- 10.03.88 C.14-03 / 14-03 (Dassault Mirage F1CE), Ala 14 (BA de Albacete), crashes in Épila (Zaragoza), shortly after taking off from Zaragoza AB bound for its base. Lieutenant Colonel José Carlos Vargas de la Rúa, ejected, although he died of his wounds.
- 13.06.89 Both pilots of C.14-32 / 14-32 (Dassault Mirage F1CE) and C.14-48 / 14-48 (Dassault Mirage F1CE), Ala 14 (BA de Albacete), they are forced to eject from their planes when the ammunition of the cannon they

Accidents and incidents of the Mirage F1 (C.14) in the Air Force

were using during an air-to-ground shooting exercise at the Bardenas Reales shooting range (Navarra) is defective; the two accidents, although caused by the same cause, were separated; both pilots, Lieutenant Colonel Sebastián Delgado Asenjo and Captain Manuel Fernández-Roca Teigell (see 10.03.82 / 15.10.90), respectively, suffered serious injuries.

- 05.07.89 CE.14-29 / 14-72 (Dassault Mirage F1BE), Ala 14 (BA de Albacete), crashes in the field of maneuvers of the Army of Chinchilla (Albacete), jumping from it Major José Luis Abad Cellini and Lieutenant Javier Román Gómez Bas, suffering less serious injuries.
- 02.02.90 CE.14-28 / 14-71 (Dassault Mirage F1BE) (see 17.12.92), Ala 14 (BA de Albacete), suffers an accident when landing on his BA, due to a failure in the left leg of the main landing gear, although it was repaired; the pilots, Lieutenant Colonel José Froilán Rodríguez Lorca and Captain Antonio Javier Taranilla Manjón, were unharmed.
- 15.10.90 C.14-39 / 14-36 (Dassault Mirage F1CE) and C.14-49 / 14-49 (Dassault Mirage F1CE), Ala14 (BA de Albacete), collide in flight over Fuensanta (Albacete), during a night interception mission; Major Faustino José Martínez Luna died on the first plane, while Major Manuel Fernández-Roca Teigell (see 10.03.82 / 13.06.89) was able to eject from its jet (C.14-49), suffering serious injuries.
- 22.05.91 C.14-61 / 46-10 (Dassault Mirage F1EE), of 462 Escuadrón, Ala 46 (BA de Gando, Gran Canaria), crashes 77 miles southeast of the Island of Gran Canaria, during an air-to-air combat training mission, Captain Rafael Sánchez Sánchez killed.
- 27.08.91 C.14-23 / 14-23 (Dassault Mirage F1CE), Ala 14 (BA de Albacete), during the approach to its airfield, crashes about 3 km from it, when it suffers a hydraulic failure, which resulted in a blockade of controls its pilot, Captain Emilio Gracia Cirujeda ejects (see 06.04. 92), who suffers minor injuries.
- 29.01.92 C.14-59 / 46-08 (Dassault Mirage F1EE), 462 Escuadrón, Ala 46 (BA de Gando, Gran Canaria), falls into the water three minutes after taking off, about 10 miles southeast of its BA, being able to jump from it Captain Jose Ignacio Pozo Diez, being rescued by an HD.21 Super Puma of the 802 Squadron , suffering minor injuries. The accident occurred due to the engine stoppage of C.14.
- 06.04.92 CE.14-30 / 14-70 (Dassault Mirage F1BE), Ala 14 (BA de Albacete), suffers a fire in take-off run from its airfield, being able to stop the plane on the runway and being extinguished by personnel of firefighters; the pilots, Captain Emilio Gracia Cirujeda (see 27.08.91) and Lieutenant Francisco Javier Martín García-Almenta, were unharmed.
- 20.07.92 C.14-19 / 14-19 (Dassault Mirage F1CE), Ala 14 (BA de Albacete), is destroyed by suffering a loss of power when starting the break for the landing, the pilot, Captain Carlos Isasi-Isasmendi Krawel, ejected, suffering minor injuries; the plane fell about ten kilometers south of it.
- 29.09.92 C.14-64 / (without numeral, which would later be 14-64) (Dassault Mirage F1EE), Ala14 (BA de Albacete), takes a maximum brakingduring landing, blocking the main landing, busting the tires and crossing the track, suffering various damages in its structure; The pilot, Captain Cándido Antonio Bernal Fuentes, was unharmed.
- 20.10.92 C.14-07 / 14-07 (Dassault Mirage F1CE) and C.14-24 / 14-24 (Dassault Mirage F1CE), Ala 14 (BA from Albacete), during a flight from its air base to Florennes (Belgium), forming part of a formation of four planes as leader and second element wingman, collide over Fontaine Les Cappy (near Cambrai, France); both pilots were ejected from their planes, the leader died (C.14-07), Major José Miguel López Merino (C.O. 141 Escuadrón), whose parachuted did not open, while the pilot of the other plane, Captain Julio de Vargas Vidal, suffered minor injuries.
- 17.12.92 CE.14-28 / 14-71 (Dassault Mirage F1BE) (see 02.02.90), Ala 14 (BA de Albacete), crashes in Minaya (Albacete) during an air-to-air mission, ejecting from it Captain José Manuel Sánchez Baeza (instructor) and Lieutenant José Antonio Bautista Castaño (student); Although the latter suffered less serious injuries, the launch sequence of Captain Sánchez Baeza failed, being killed.
- 05.07.95 C.14-88 / 14-88 (Dassault Mirage F1C), Ala14 (BA de Albacete), suffered a runway in its airfiled, being subsequently recovered.
- 29.08.95 C.14-67 / 14-67 (Dassault Mirage F1CE), Ala14 (BA from Albacete), engage the braking barrier when landing on its BA, light damage.
- __. 04.96 CE.14C-85 / 11-70 (Dassault Mirage F1DDA, 539), of Ala11 (BA de Manises, Valencia), quickly repaired due to a fire in previous flight, having been able to land the pilots with it.
- 12.06.97 C.14-09 / 14-09 (Dassault Mirage F1CE), attached to Ala 46 (BA de Gando, Gran Canaria), crashes near Ligneuville (Belgium), ejecting his pilot, Captain Ricardo Guerra García, due to an engine stoppage. The plane had taken off from Norvenich AB (Germany), during the course of the CENTRAL ENTRERPRISE exercise, in a formation

of six Spanish F1, but when warning the pilot failures in the proper functioning of his plane he left the formation, returning to this airfield, although he finally had to eject. Captain Guerra avoided a high voltage line before hitting the plane against the ground and passed under another power line.

- 05.01.98 C.14-51 / 14-51 (Dassault Mirage F1CE), Ala 14 (BA de Albacete), during a test of taxiing and acceleration on land in it air base, goes off the runway, catching fire, the pilot being unharmed, Lieutenant Felipe Gómez Ruiz.
- 20.03.02 C.14-62 / 14-35 (Dassault Mirage F1M), Ala 14 (BA de Albacete), crashes in the vicinity of the Giribaile reservoir (Carrena, Jaen), by Lieutenant Fernando Negrete Usón ejected (see 20.01.09), who into the water of the reservoir, being rescued by civilian personnel that was in the area and members of the Civil Guard, being seriously injured.
- 10.06.02 C.14-52 / 14-52 (Dassault Mirage F1M), Ala 14 (BA de Albacete), engages in the braking barrier when landing on a night flight in itsairfield, having to be struck of charge; without consequences for his pilot, captain Rafael Muñoz Delmás.
- 19.06.02 C.14-69 / 14-41 (Dassault Mirage F1M), Ala 14 (BA de Albacete), catches fire at the head of the runway, shortly before taking off, struck of charge; without consequences for its pilot, Captain Francisco Javier Hípola Fernández.
- 28.06.02 C.14-50 / 14-28 (Dassault Mirage F1M), Ala 14 (BA de Albacete), landed with the undercarriage retracted, leaving the track, struck of charge. The pilot, Lieutenant José Alberto García Gómez, was seriously injured.
- 04.05.04 C.14-71 / 14-43 (Dassault Mirage F1M), Ala 14 (BA de Albacete), crashes at Arteaga de Arriba (Peñascosa, Albacete), the pilot Captain Miguel Alejandro Esteban Calonge, was killed.
- 30.05.05 C.14-01 / 14-01 (Dassault Mirage F1M) (see 30.03.76 / 10.05.83), Ala 14 (BA de Albacete), crashes in the vicinity of Neuburg (Germany), and Lieutenant Ricardo Vidal Díaz ejected safely.
- 05.07.05 C.14-40 / 14-21 (Dassault Mirage F1M), Ala 14 (BA de Albacete), when landing, the landing gear is retracted and the jet was repaired later.
- 21.03.06 C.14-22 / 14-15 (Dassault Mirage F1M), Ala 14 (BA de Albacete), crashes in La Roda (Albacete), Captain Pedro Martínez Monleón ejected suffering minor injuries.
- 20.01.09 CE.14-31 / 14-72 (Dassault Mirage F1BE (M)) and C.14-40 / 14-21 (Dassault Mirage F1M), Ala 14 (BA de Albacete), collide in flight near Ossa de Montiel (Albacete), Captain Fernando Negrete Usón (see 20.03.02) and Lieutenant Roberto Carlos Álvarez Cubillas on the first plane and Captain Jerónimo José Carbonell Rodriguez in the second, were killed.

Dassault Mirage F1 Ejército del Aire			
Serial	Variant	Side number	Notes
C.14-01	F1CE(M)	141-01 > 14-01	w/o 30.05.2005 Neuburg (Germany); pilot ejected
C.14-2	F1CE	141-02	w/o 04.01.1977 Lezuza (Albacete); pilot killed
C.14-03	F1CE	141-03 > 14-03	w/o 10.03.1988 Épila (Zaragoza); pilot killed
C.14-04	F1CE(M)	141-04 > 14-04 > 14-02	(wfu 2009)
C.14-05	F1CE	141-05	w/o 14.09.1984 Casas de Haro (Albacete); pilot killed
C.14-06	F1CE(M)	141-06 > 14-06 > 14-03	(wfu 2009)
C.14-07	F1CE	141-07 > 14-07	w/o 20.09.1992 Fontaine les Cappy (France); pilot killed
C.14-08	F1CE(M)	141-08 > 14-08 > (14-04)	(wfu 2006); gate guardian racing track (Albacete)
C.14-09	F1CE	141-09 > 14-09	w/o 12.06.1997 Ligneuville (Belgium); pilot ejected
C.14-10	F1CE(M)	141-10 > 14-10 > 14-05	(wfu 2010)
C.14-11	F1CE(M)	141-11 > 14-11 > 14-06	(wfu 2008)
C.14-12	F1CE	141-12	w/o 11.10.1983 offshore Motril (Granada); pilot ejected
C.14-13	F1CE(M)	141-13 > 14-13 > 14-07	
C.14-14	F1CE(M)	141-14 > 14-14 > 14-08	(wfu 2005)
C.14-15	F1CE(M)	141-15 > 14-15 > 14-09	(wfu 2010)
C.14-16	F1CE(M)	141-16 > 14-16 > 14-10	(wfu 2010)
C.14-17	F1CE(M)	141-17 > 14-17 > 14-11	
C.14-18	F1CE(M)	141-18 > 14-18 > 14-12	
C.14-19	F1CE	141-19 > 14-19	w/o 20.07.1992 near Los Llanos aB, piloto ejected
C.14-20	F1CE(M)	141-20 > 14-20 > 14-13	(wfu 2010)
C.14-21	F1CE(M)	141-21 > 14-21 > 14-14	(wfu 2010)
C.14-22	F1CE(M)	141-22 > 14-22 > 14-15	w/o 21.03.2006 La Roda (Albacete); pilot ejected
C.14-23	F1CE	141-23 > 141-49 > 14-23	w/o 27.08.1991 near BA Albacete; pilot ejected
C.14-24	F1CE	141-24 > 142-25 > 14-24	w/o 20.09.1992 Fontaine les Cappy (France); pilot ejected
C.14-25	F1CE	141-25 > 142-26	w/o 29.01.1996 El Ballestero (Albacete); pilot killed
CE.14-26	F1BE	141-23	w/o 07.04.1981 Villa de Ves (Albacete); pilotos ejected
CE.14-27	F1BE(M)	141-24 > 14-70 > 14-74 > 14-70	
CE.14-28	F1BE	142-47 > 14-71 > 14-75	w/o 17.12.1992 Minaya (Albacete); a pilot killed, the other ejected

Accidents and incidents of the Mirage F1 (C.14) in the Air Force

Dassault Mirage F1 Ejército del Aire			
Serial	Variant	Side number	Notes
CE.14-29	F1BE	142-48 > 14-72	w/o 05.07.1989 Chinchilla (Albacete); pilots ejected
CE.14-30	**F1BE(M)**	**462-23 > 46-70 > 14-76 > 14-71**	
CE.14-31	F1BE(M)	462-24 > 46-71 > 14-77 > 14-72	w/o 20.01.2009 Ossa de Montiel (Albacete); pilots killed
C.14-32	F1CE	142-27 > 14-32	w/o 13.06.1989 Bardenas weapons range; pilot ejected
C.14-33	F1CE(M)	142-28 > 14-33 > 14-16	(wfu 2004); gate guardian at Los Llanos AB as "C.14-91/14-91"
C.14-34	F1CE(M)	142-29 > 14-34 > 14-17	(wfu 2004); gate guardian at Universidad Politécnica Valencia
C.14-35	F1CE	142-30	w/o 27.02.85 Villasequilla de Yepes (Toledo); pilot killed
C.14-36	F1CE(M)	142-31 > 14-36 > 14-18	(wfu 2010)
C.14-37	**F1CE(M)**	**142-32 > 14-37 > 14-19**	
C.14-38	**F1CE(M)**	**142-33 > 14-38 > 14-20**	
C.14-39	F1CE	142-34 > 14-39	w/o 15.10.1990 Fuensanta (Albacete); pilot killed
C.14-40	F1CE(M)	142-35 > 14-40 > 14-21	w/o 20.01.2009 Ossa de Montiel (Albacete); pilot killed
C.14-41	**F1CE(M)**	**142-36 > 14-41 > 14-22**	
C.14-42	**F1CE(M)**	**142-37 > 14-42 > 14-23**	
C.14-43	F1CE(M)	142-38 > 14-43 > 14-24	(wfu 2010)
C.14-44	F1CE(M)	142-39 > 14-44 > 14-25	(wfu 2010)
C.14-45	**F1CE(M)**	**142-40 > 14-45 > 14-26**	
C.14-46	F1CE	142-41	w/o 28.09.1982 Alhama de Granada (Murcia); pilot ejected
C.14-47	F1CE(M)	142-42 > 14-47 > 14-27	wfu 2005, gate guardian Paterna (Valencia)
C.14-48	F1CE	142-43 > 14-48	w/o 13.06.1989 Bardenas weapons range; pilot ejected
C.14-49	F1CE	142-44 > 14-49	w/o 15.10.1990 Fuensanta (Albacete); pilot ejected
C.14-50	F1CE(M)	142-45 > 14-35 > 14-50 > 14-28	wfu 2002 take-off accident Los Llanos aB; pilot safe
C.14-51	F1CE	142-46 > 14-46 > 14-51	wfu 1998 landing accident Los Llanos AB; pilot safe
C.14-52	F1EE(M)	462-01 > 46-01 > 14-52 > (14-29)	wfu 2002 landing accident; pilot safe
C.14-53	F1EE	462-02	w/o 25.06.1985 offshore Gran Canaria Island; pilot killed
C.14-54	**F1EE(M)**	**462-03 > 46-03 > 14-54 > 14-30**	
C.14-55	F1EE	462-04	w/o 25.06.1985 offshore Gran Canaria Island; pilot ejected
C.14-56	**F1EE(M)**	**462-05 > 46-05 > 14-56 > 14-31**	
C.14-57	**F1EE(M)**	**462-06 > 46-06 > 14-57 > 14-32**	
C.14-58	F1EE(M)	462-07 > 46-07 > 14-58 > 14-33	w/o 10.09.2009 Cazorla (Jaen); pilot ejected
C.14-59	F1EE	462-08 > 46-08	w/o 29.01.1992 offshore Gran Canaria Island; pilot ejected
C.14-60	**F1EE(M)**	**462-09 > 46-09 > 14-60 > 14-34**	
C.14-61	F1EE	462-10 > 46-10	w/o 22.05.1991 offshore Gran Canaria Island; pilot killed
C.14-62	F1EE(M)	462-11 > 46-11 > 14-62 > 14-35	w/o 20.03.2002 Giribaile dam (Jaen); pilot ejected
C.14-63	**F1EE(M)**	**462-12 > 46-12 > 14-63 > 14-36**	
C.14-64	**F1EE(M)**	**462-13 > 46-13 > 14-64 > 14-37**	
C.14-65	F1EE	462-14	w/o 01.06.1984 Gando AB, Gran Canaria Is. Pilot safe
C.14-66	F1EE(M)	462-15 > 46-15 > 14-66 > 14-38	(wfu) 2010
C.14-67	**F1EE(M)**	**462-16 > 46-16 > 14-67 > 14-39**	
C.14-68	**F1EE(M)**	**462-17 > 46-17 > 14-68 > 14-40**	
C.14-69	F1EE(M)	462-18 > 46-18 > 14-69 > 14-41	w/o 2002 take-off accident Los Llanos AB; pilot safe
C.14-70	**F1EE(M)**	**462-19 > 46-19 > 14-70 > 14-42**	
C.14-71	F1EE(M)	462-20 > 46-20 > 14-71 > 14-43	w/o 04.05.2004 Peñascosa (Albacete); pilot killed
C.14-72	**F1EE(M)**	**462-21 > 46-21 > 14-72 > 14-44**	
C.14-73	F1EE(M)	462-22 > 46-22 > 14-73 > 14-45	(wfu 2010)
C.14C-74	F1EDA	11-01 > 14-50	(wfu 2002); gate guardian, Zaragoza AB
C.14C-75	F1EDA	11-02 > 14-51	(wfu 2002); gate guardina Lanzarote airfield
C.14C-76	F1EDA	11-03 > 14-52	(wfu 2002); gate guardan Socuéllamos (Ciudad Real)
C.14C-77	F1EDA	11-04 > 14-53	(wfu 2002); Ejército del Aire Museum, Cuatro Vientos, Madrid
C.14C-78	F1EDA	11-05 > 14-54	(wfu 2002); Ejército del Aire Museum, Cuatro Vientos, Madrid
C.14C-79	F1EDA	11-06 > 14-55	(wfu 2002); gate guardian, Albacete civilian airport
C.14C-80	F1EDA	11-07 > 14-56	(wfu 2002)
C.14C-81	F1EDA	11-08 > 14-57	(wfu 2002); gate guardian Albacete Air Depot
C.14C-82	F1EDA	11-09 > 14-58	(wfu 2002); gate guardian at Los Llanos AB as "C.14-01/14-01"
C.14C-83	F1EDA	11-10 > 14-59	(wfu 2002); gate guardian Tablada airfield, Seville
(C.14C-84)	F1EDA	---	(Not delivered, w/o while still in service with the Qatar Emiri AF)
CE.14C-85	F1DDA	11-70 > 14-74	(wfu 2002); sold to the Royal Jordanian Air Force, serial 118
CE.14C-86	F1DDA	11-71 > 14-75	(wfu 2002)
CE.14-87	F1B(M)	14-76 > 14-73	(wfu 2008)
C.14-88	F1C(M)	14-88 > 14-46	(wfu 2008)
C.14-89	F1C(M)	14-89 > 14-47	(wfu 2010)
C.14-90	F1C(M)	14-90 > 14-48	(wfu 2008)
C.14-91	F1C(M)	14-91 > 14-49	(wfu 2008)

M – for Modernizado (upgraded)
Bold: Survivors sold to Draken International or displayed as gate guardians and the Air Force Museum
With special thanks to Jose Manuel Santaner for his help in drawing this box

The following illustrations show the Mirage F1AZ, a ground attack optimized variant for the South African Air Force, as well as a Spanish Mirage F1CE, mainly showing the details of the Martin Baker Mk.6 "zero-zero" ejection seat. [Author's collection]

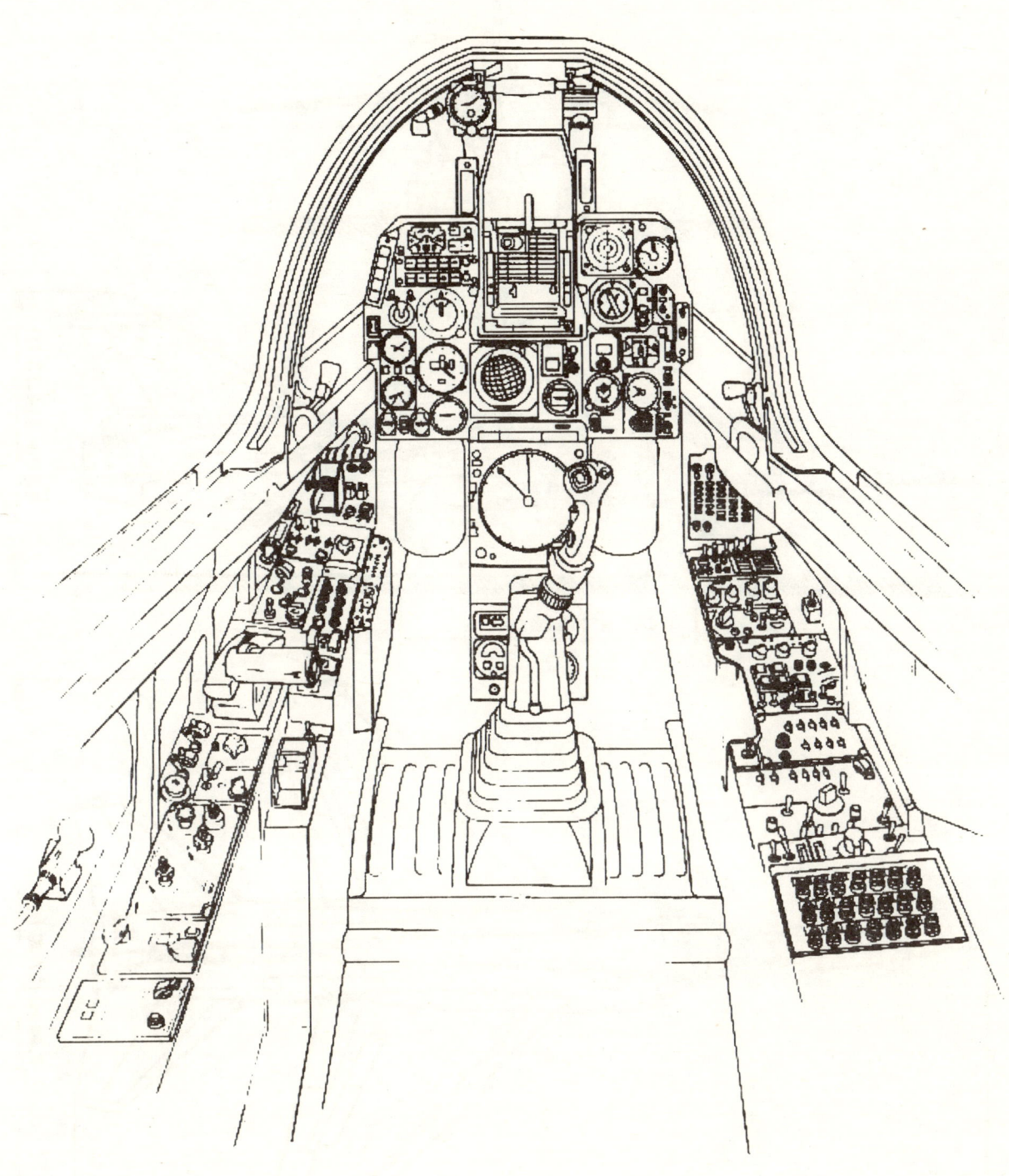

COCKPIT LAYOUT
(POST/SAAF/MOD/MIR/151, 187, 521)

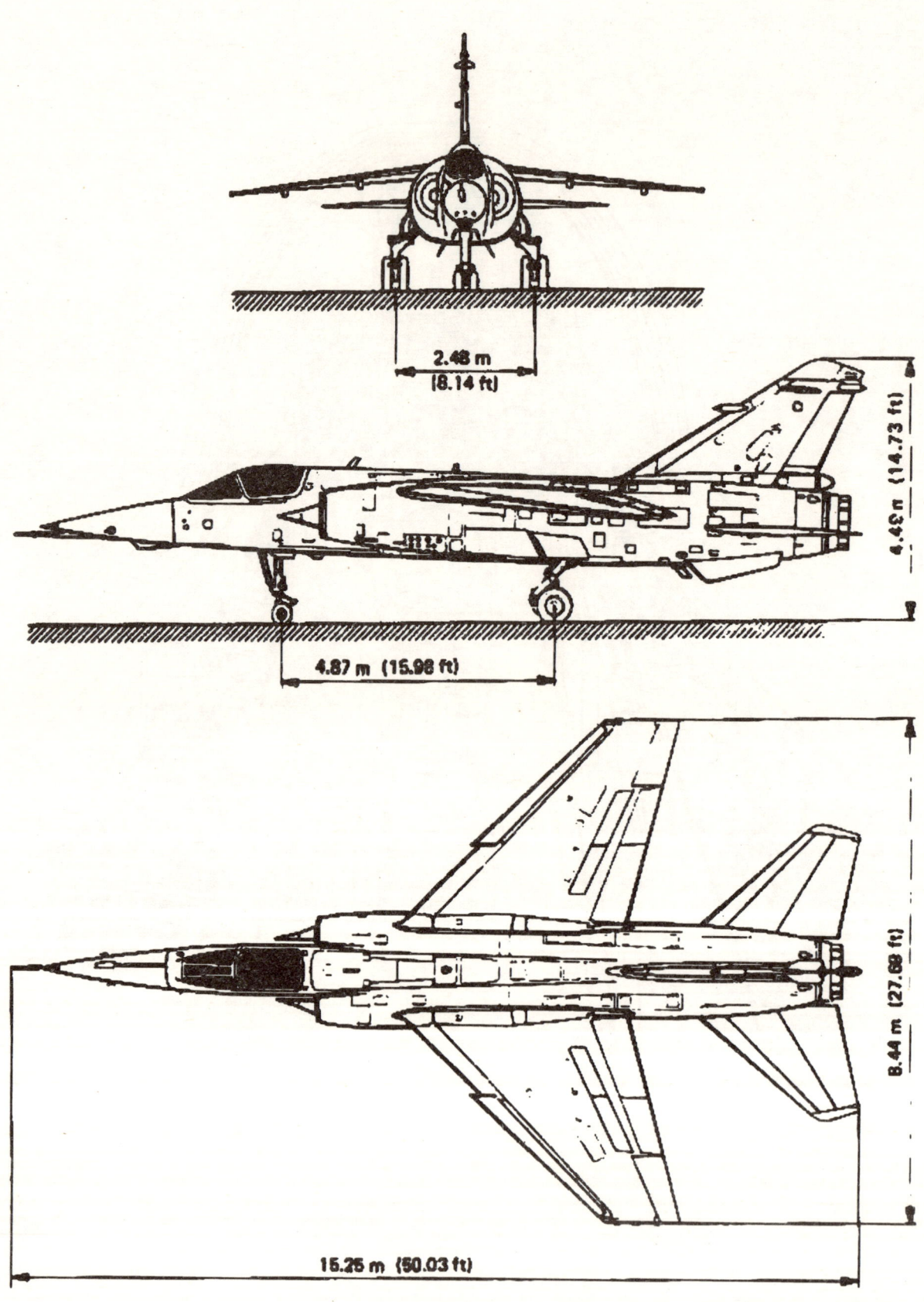

FIGURE 1 - THREE-VIEW DRAWING

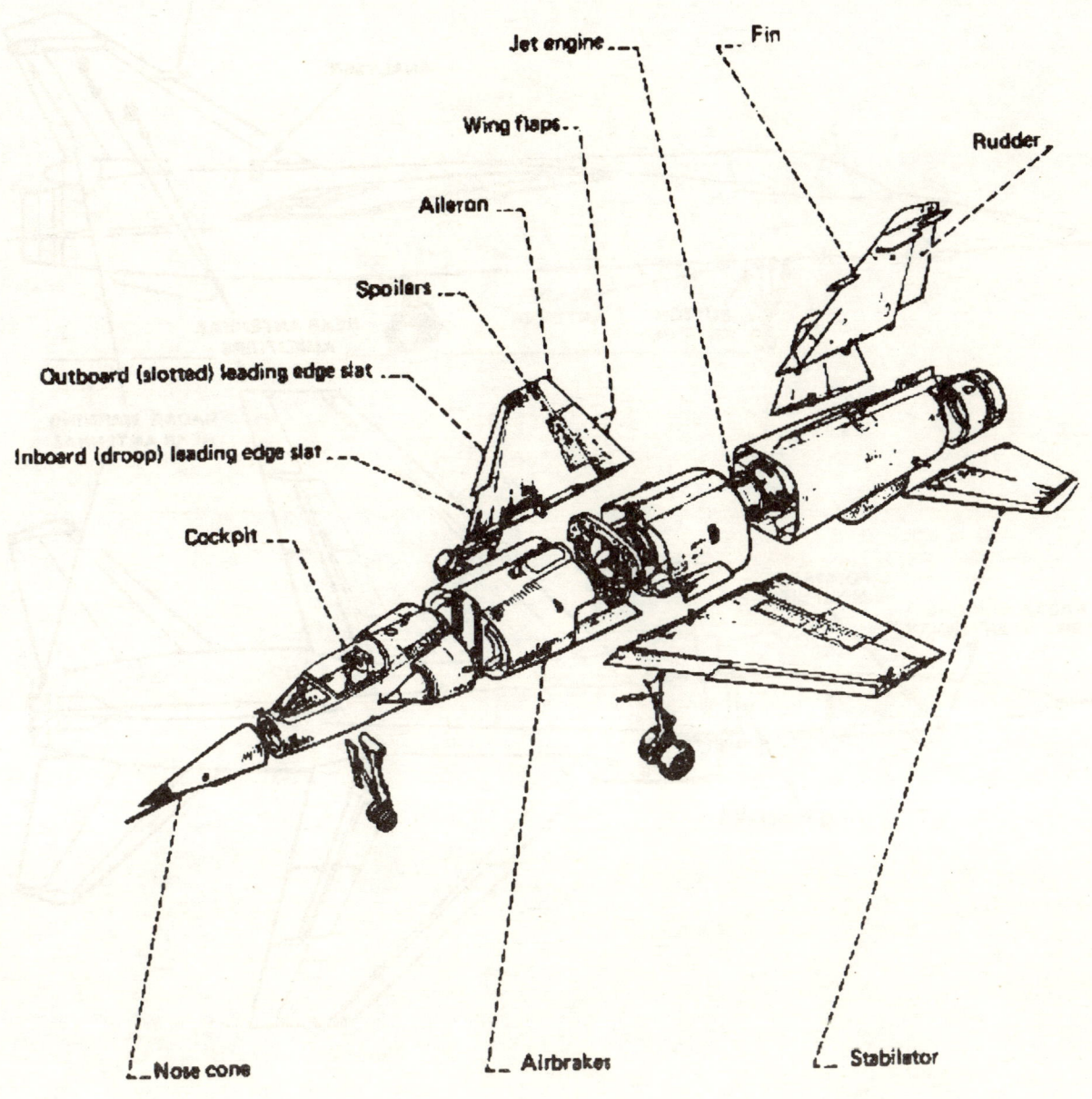

FIGURE 3 - MAJOR COMPONENTS

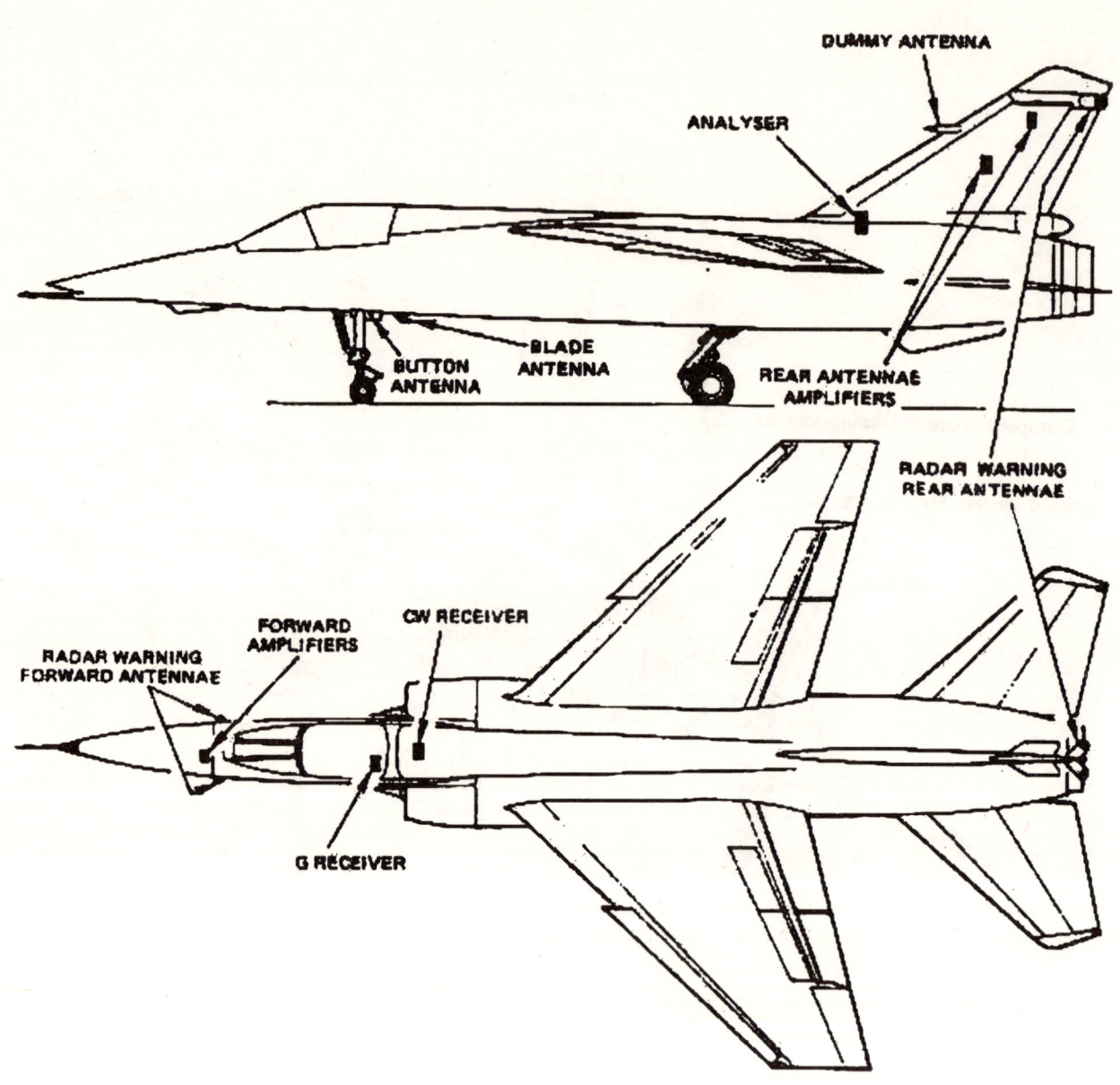

**FIGURE 4A GENERAL LAYOUT RADAR WARNING
(POST/SAAF/MOD/MIR/187)**

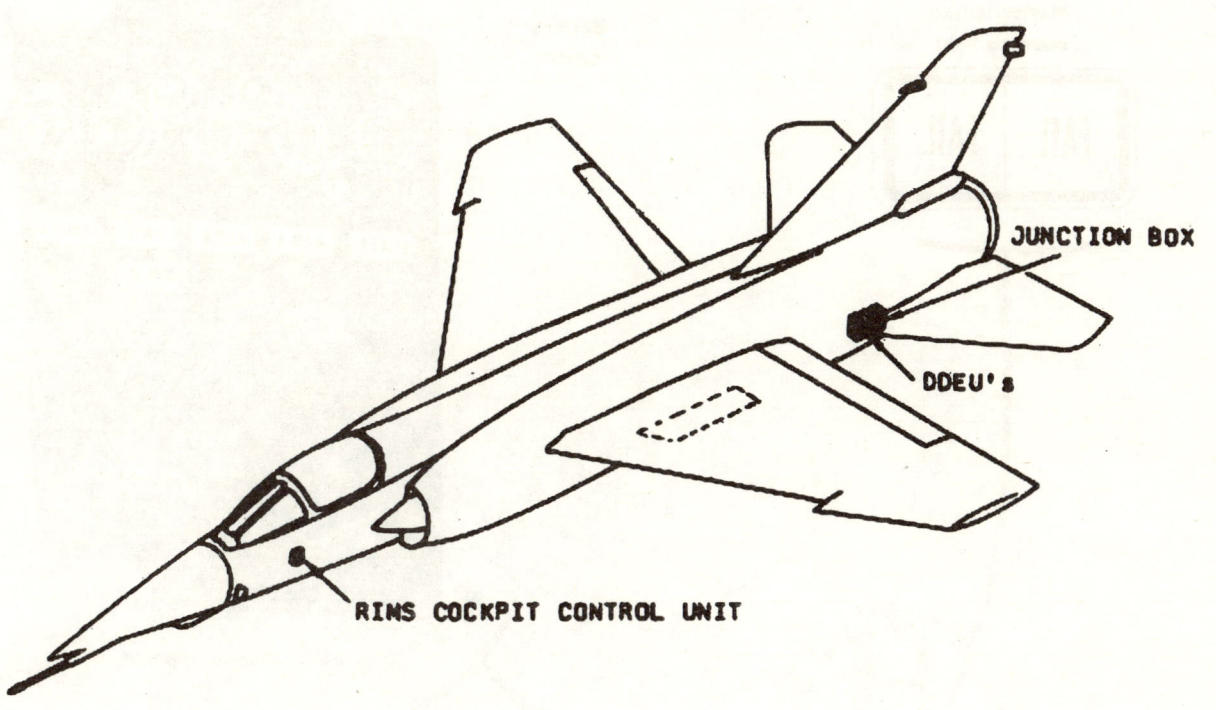
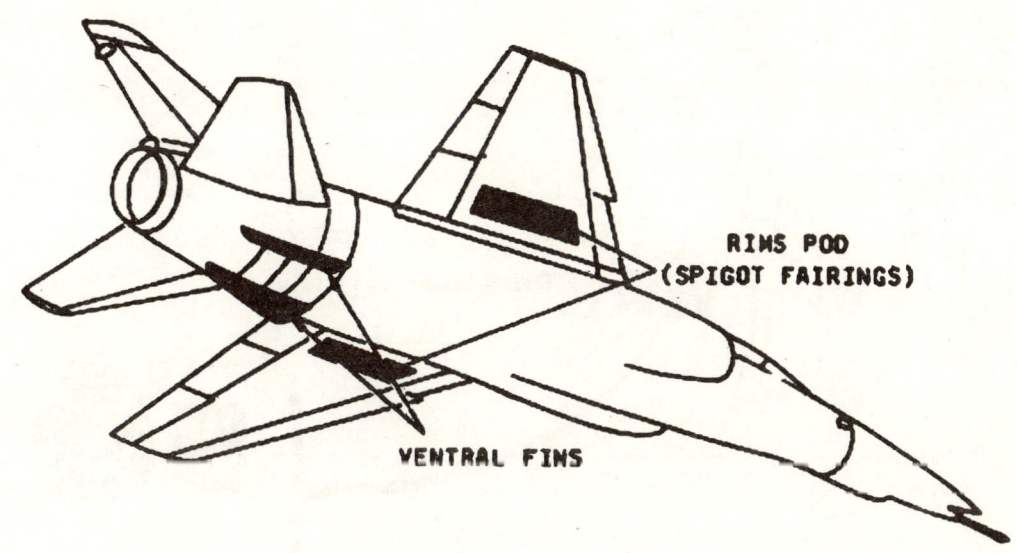

**FIGURE 4B RADAR AND INFRA-RED MISLEADING SYSTEM
(POST/SAAF/MODS/MIR 151, 521)**

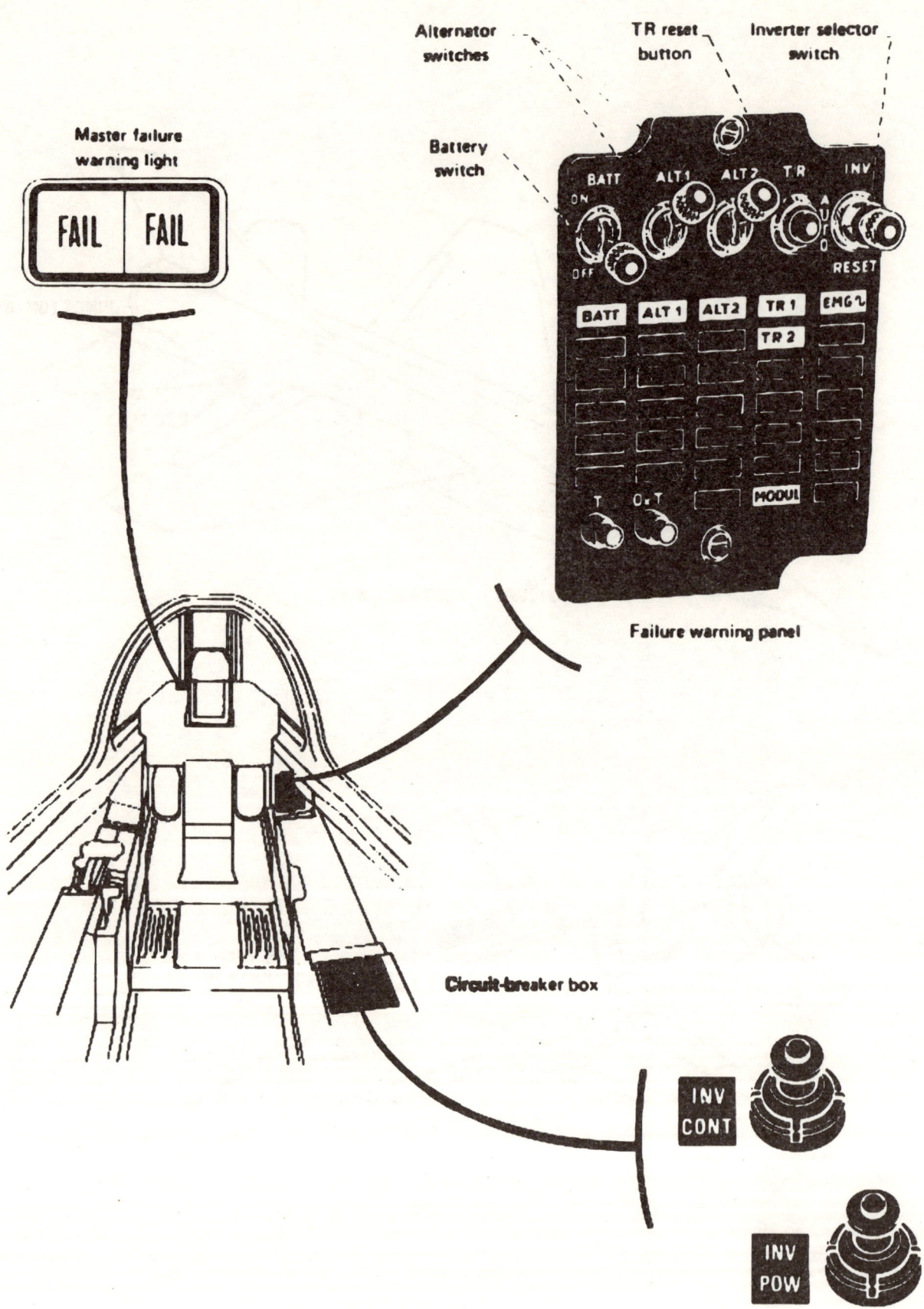

FIGURE 4 – ELECTRICAL SYSTEM CONTROLS AND INDICATORS

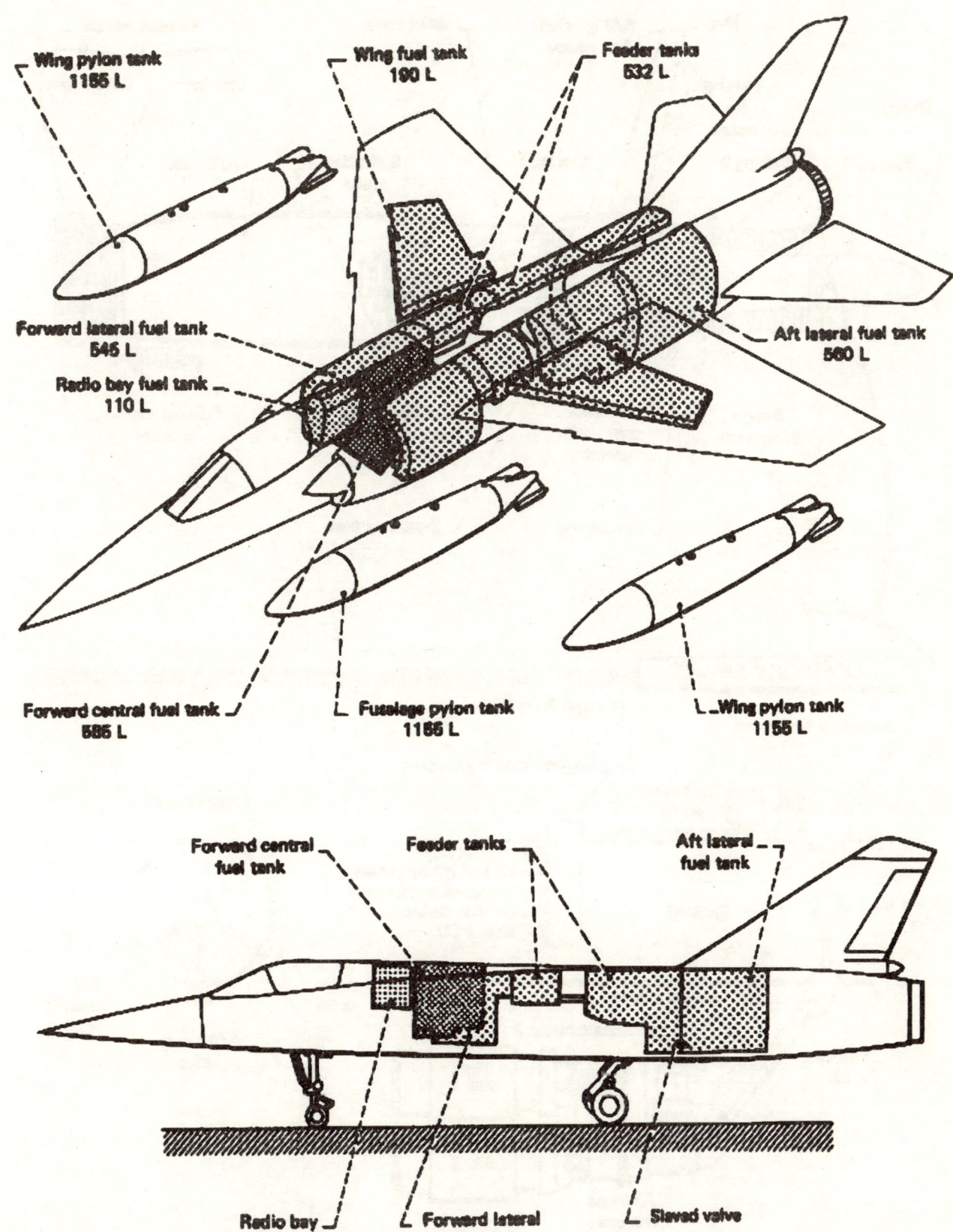

FIGURE 2M – FUEL TANK ARRANGEMENT

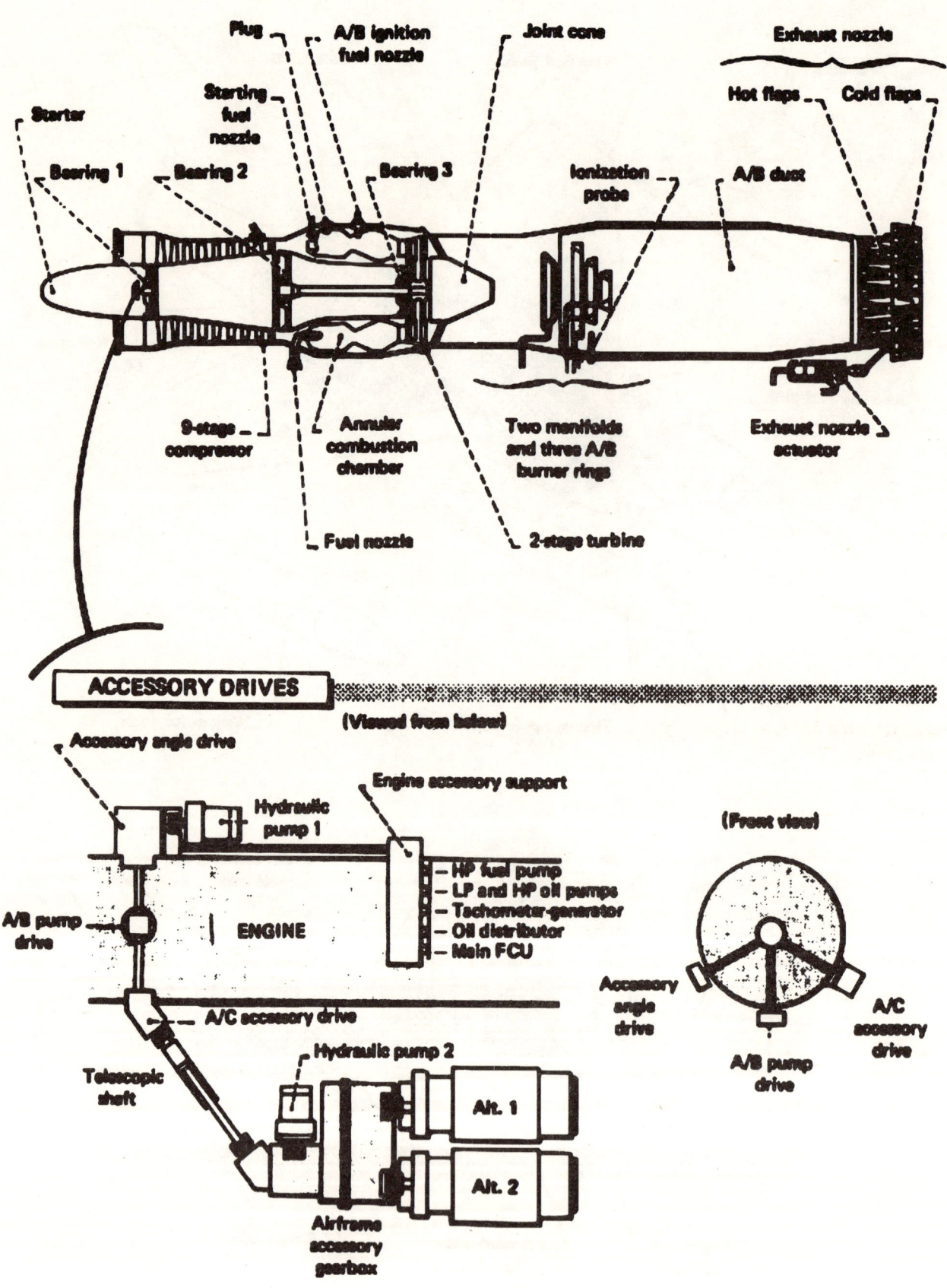

FIGURE 1 – ATAR 9K 50 JET ENGINE

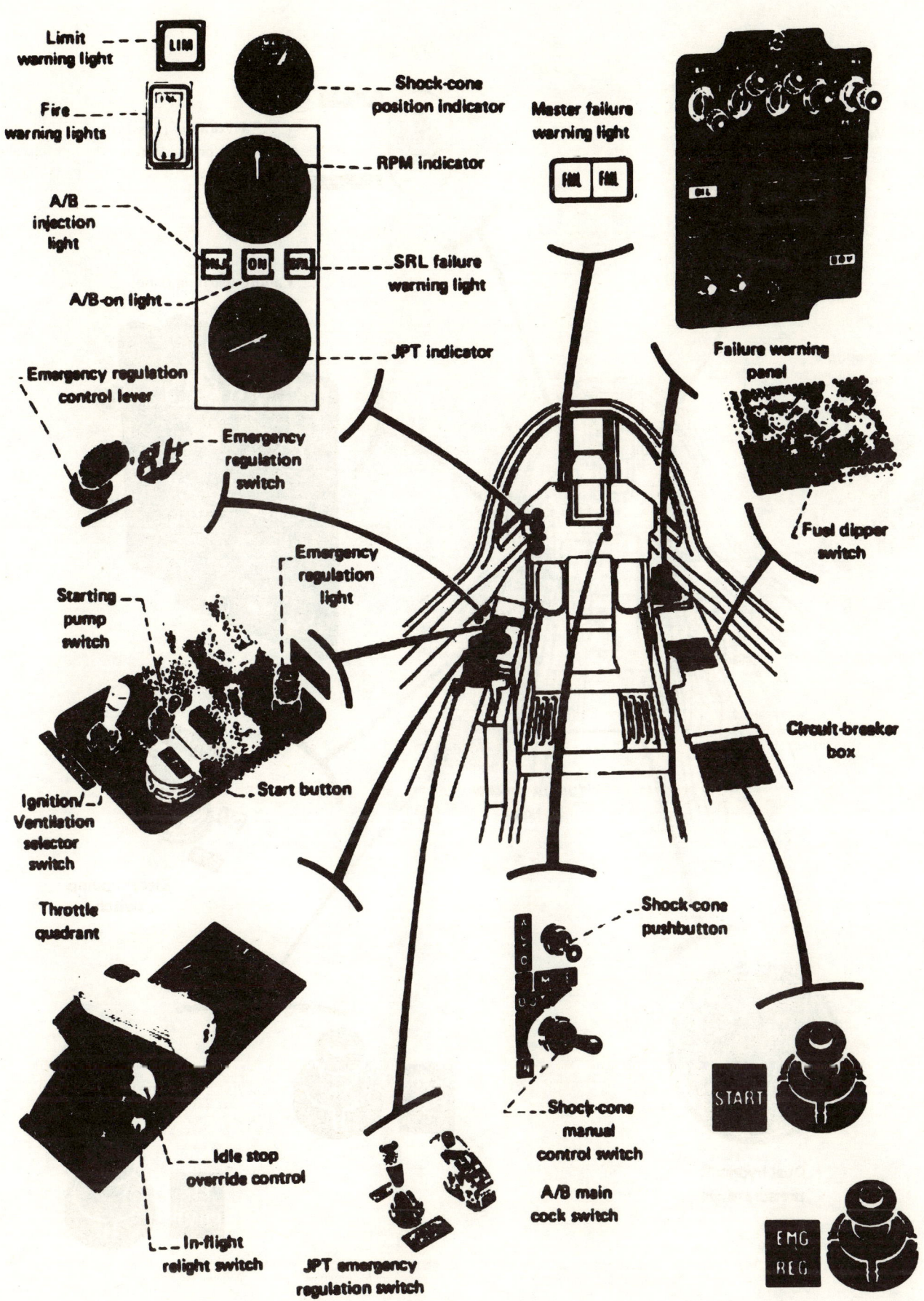

FIGURE 3 – ENGINE CONTROLS AND INDICATORS

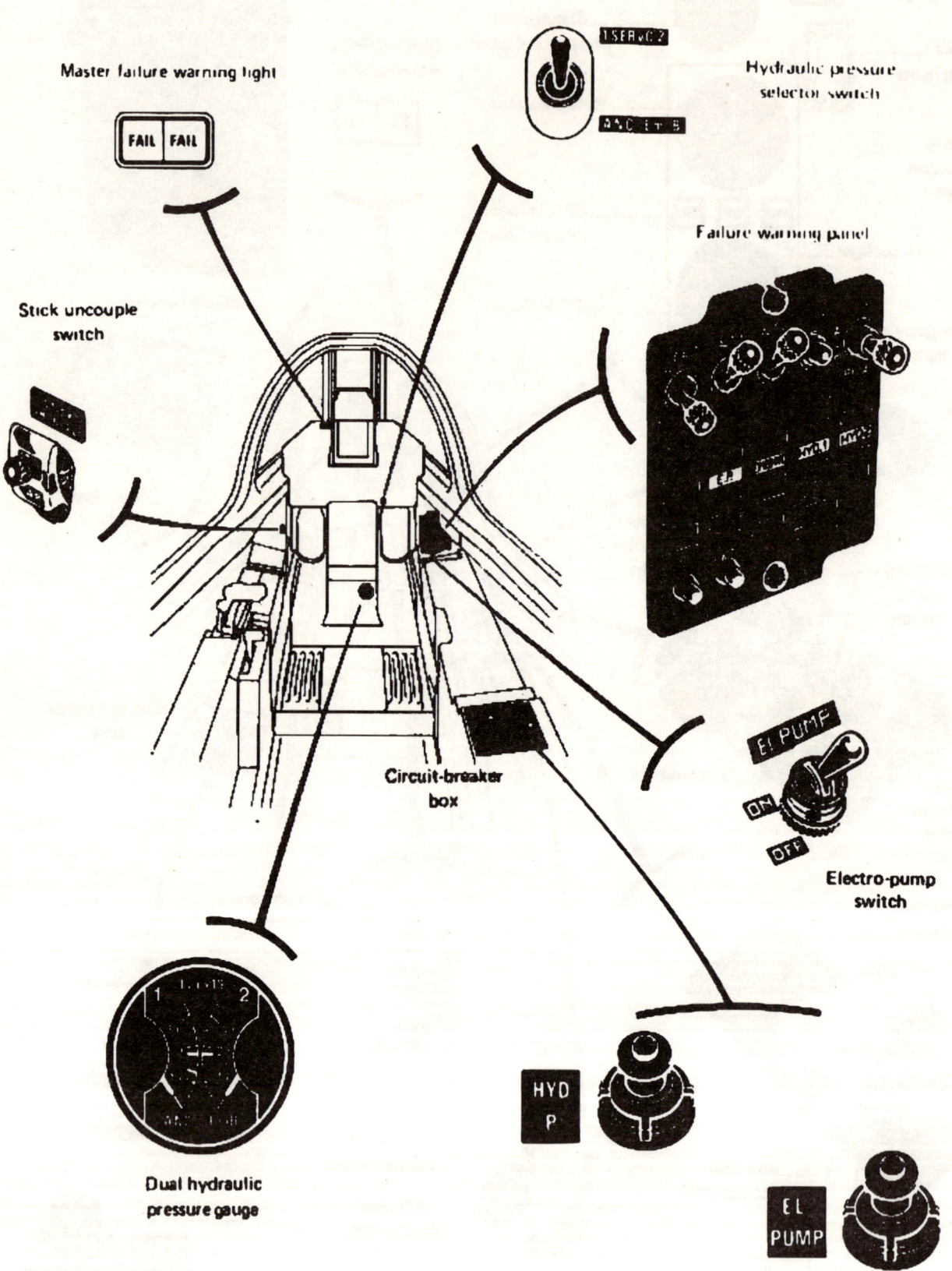

FIGURE 2 - HYDRAULIC SYSTEM CONTROLS AND INDICATORS

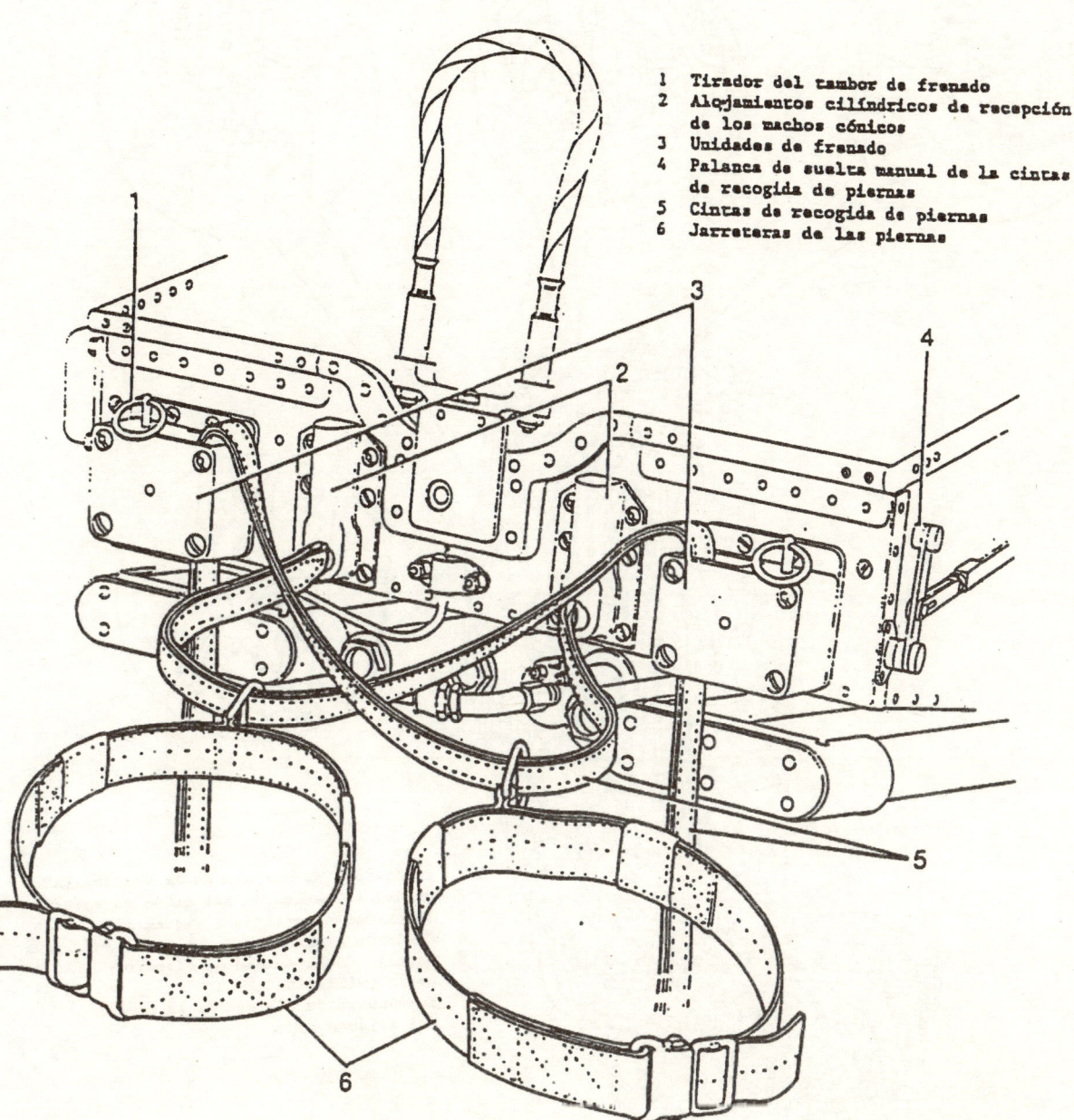

1. Tirador del tambor de frenado
2. Alojamientos cilíndricos de recepción de los machos cónicos
3. Unidades de frenado
4. Palanca de suelta manual de la cintas de recogida de piernas
5. Cintas de recogida de piernas
6. Jarreteras de las piernas

FIG.11 JARRETERAS

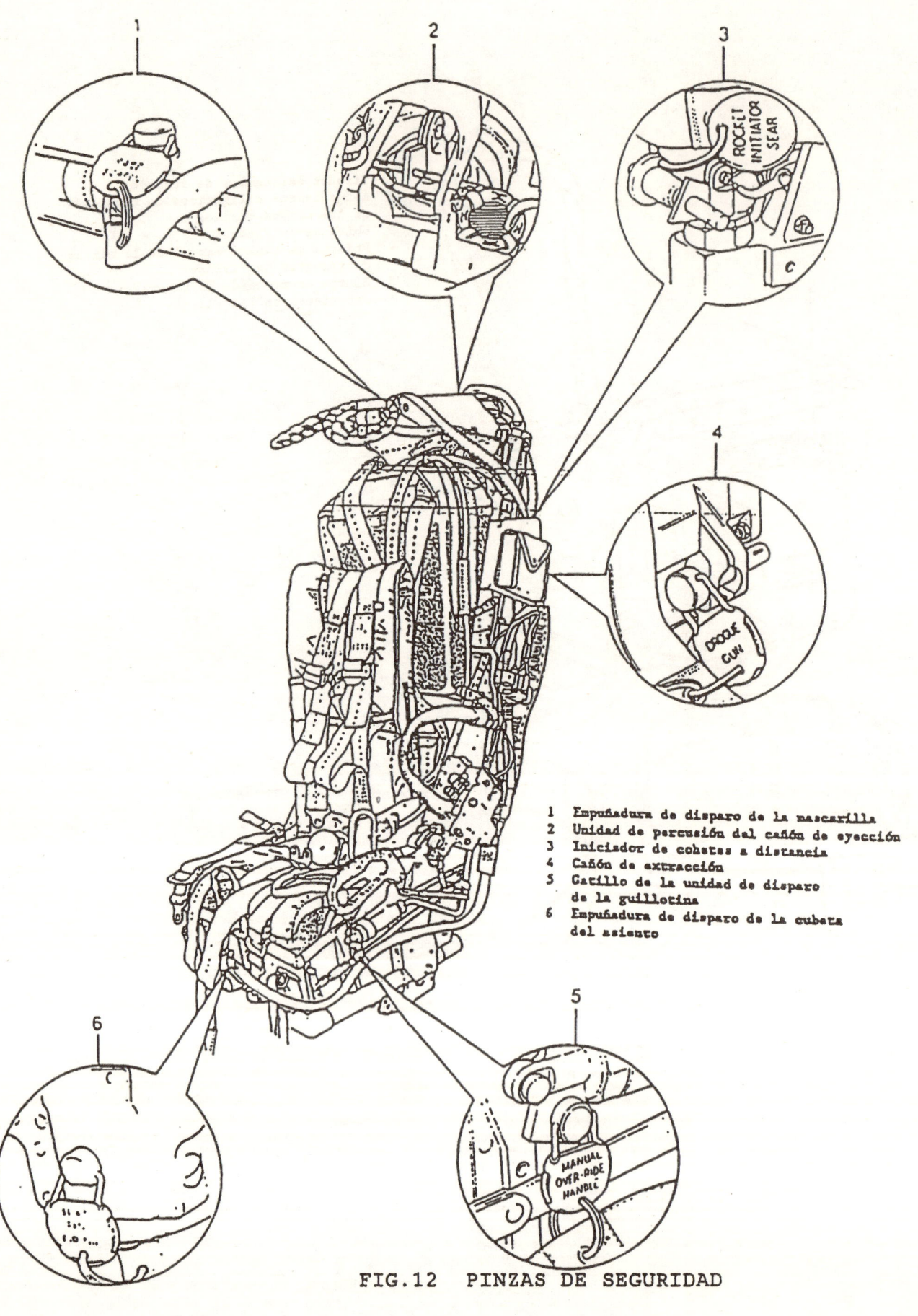

1 Empuñadura de disparo de la mascarilla
2 Unidad de percusión del cañón de eyección
3 Iniciador de cohetes a distancia
4 Cañón de extracción
5 Gatillo de la unidad de disparo de la guillotina
6 Empuñadura de disparo de la cubeta del asiento

FIG.12 PINZAS DE SEGURIDAD

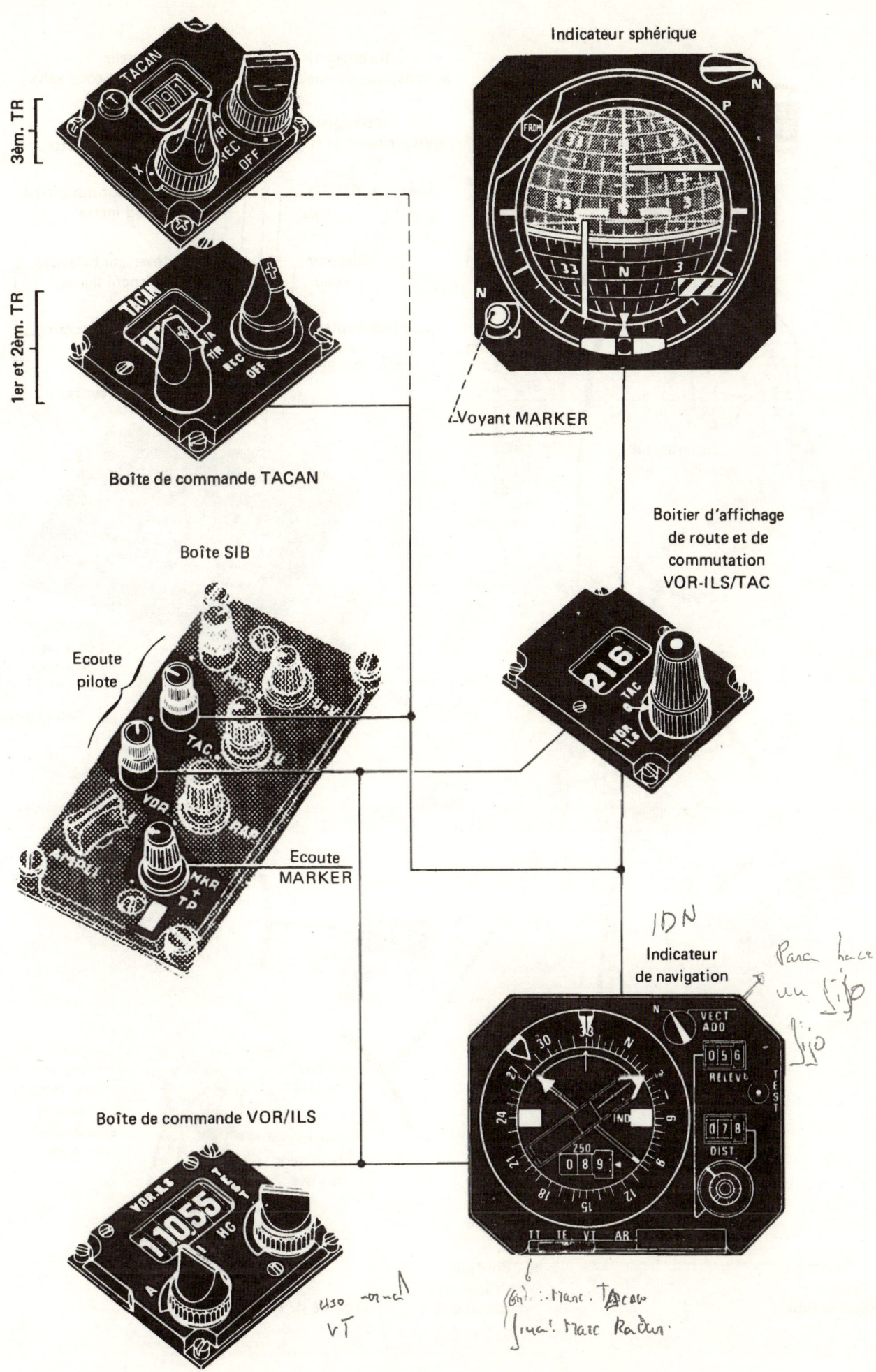

FIGURE 2 - ENSEMBLE DE NAVIGATION

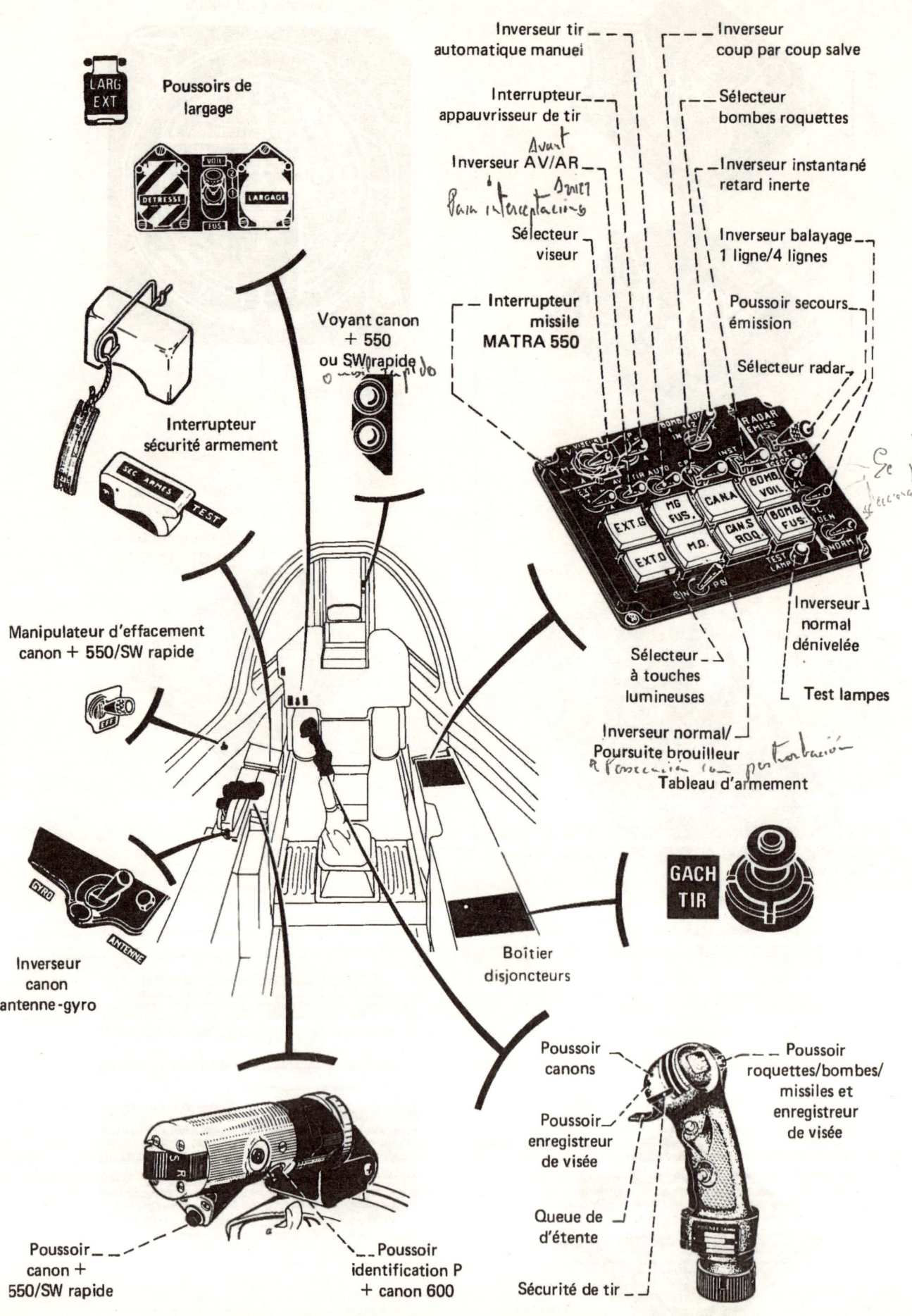

FIGURE 1 – COMMANDES ET CONTROLES DE L'ARMEMENT

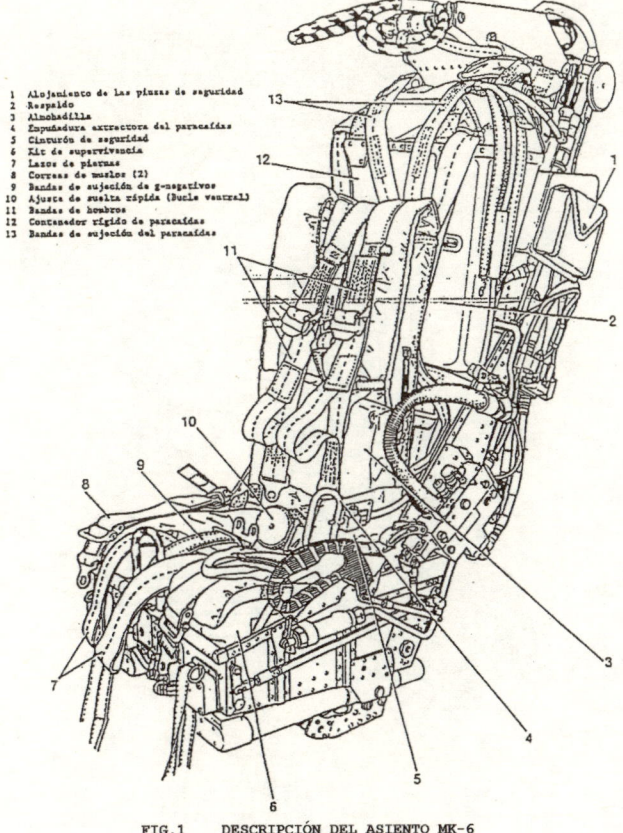

FIG.1 DESCRIPCIÓN DEL ASIENTO MK-6

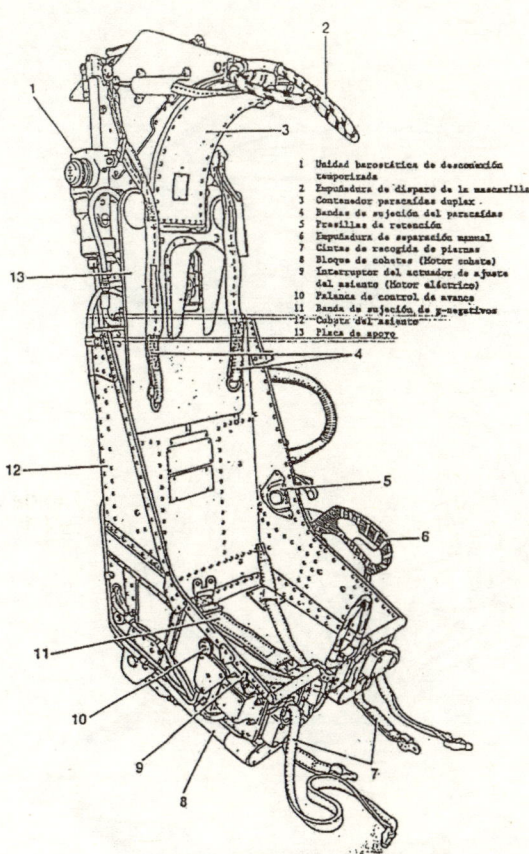

FIG.2 VISTA DERECHA DEL BAQUET

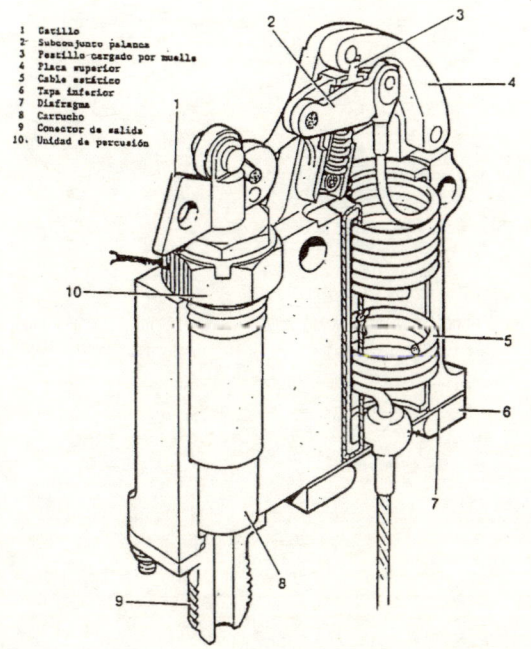

FIG.4 CORDON INICIADOR MOTOR COHETE

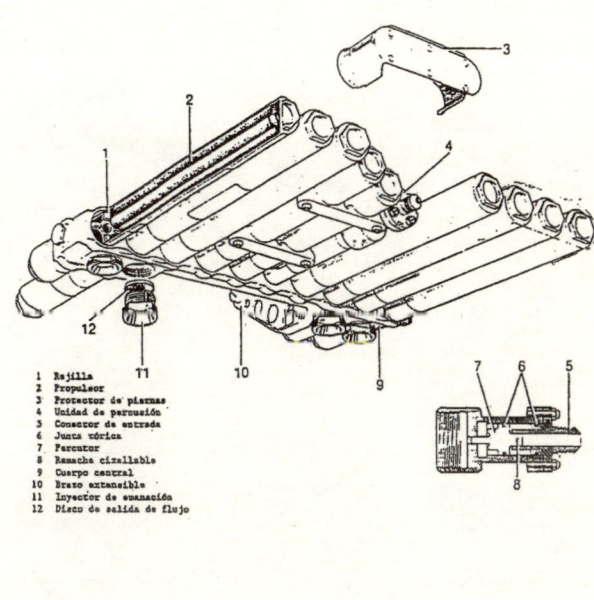

FIG.6 MOTOR COHETE: TUBOS IMPULSORES

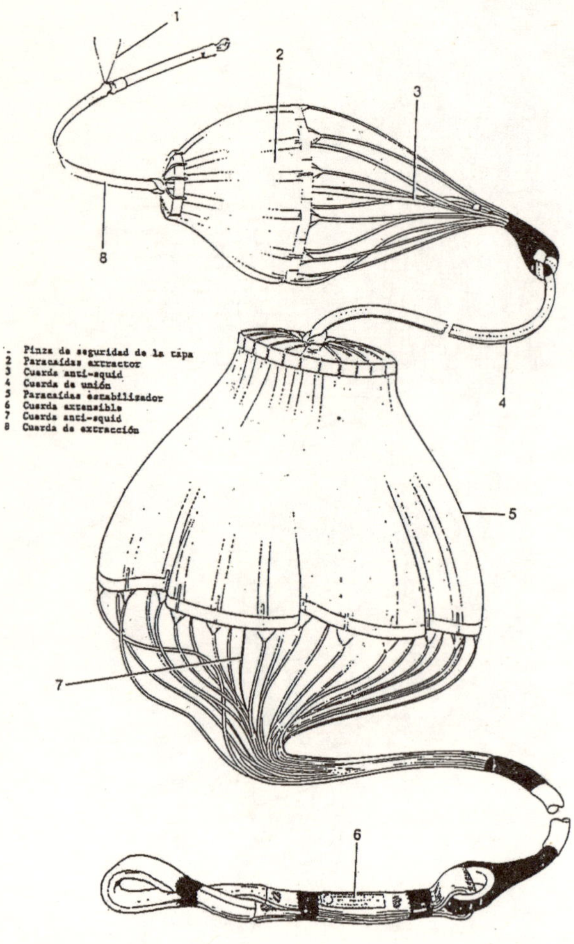

1 Pinza de seguridad de la tapa
2 Paracaídas extractor
3 Cuerda anti-squid
4 Cuerda de unión
5 Paracaídas estabilizador
6 Cuerda extensible
7 Cuerda anti-squid
8 Cuerda de extracción

FIG.7 CONJUNTO PARACAIDAS DUPLEX (EXTRACTORES)

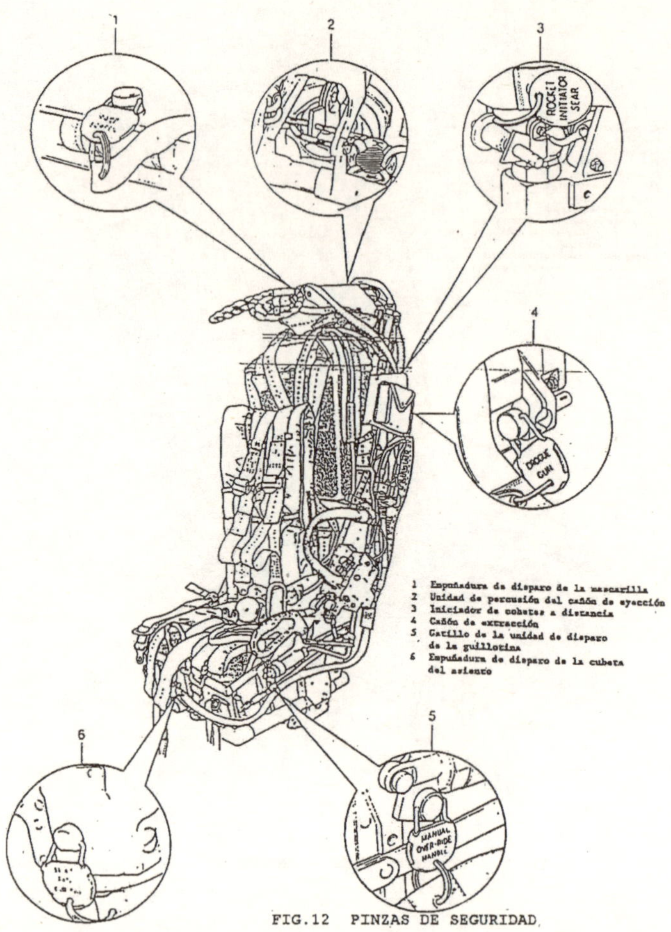

ROCKET INITIATOR SEAR
DROGUE GUN
MANUAL OVER-RIDE HANDLE
1 Empuñadura de disparo de la mascarilla
2 Unidad de percusión del cañón de eyección
3 Iniciador de cohetes a distancia
4 Cañón de extracción
5 Gatillo de la unidad de disparo de la guillotina
6 Empuñadura de disparo de la cubeta del asiento

FIG.12 PINZAS DE SEGURIDAD

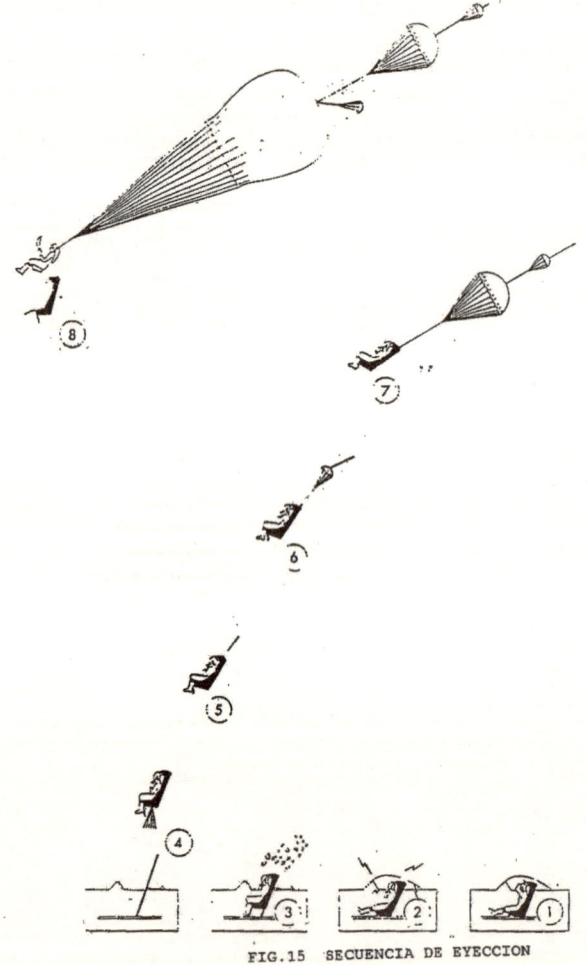

FIG.15 SECUENCIA DE EYECCION

30MF of EC 2/30 "Normandie-Niemen", May 1976

FAE-804 of Escuadron de Combate 2110, Fuerza Aerea Ecuatoriana, March 1979

Painted by Anastasios Polychronis

139 of 114 Pteriga Mahis, Hellenic Air Force, May 1979

12YO of EC 1/12 "Cambresis", September 1981

Painted by Anastasios Polychronis

Painted by Anastasios Polychronis

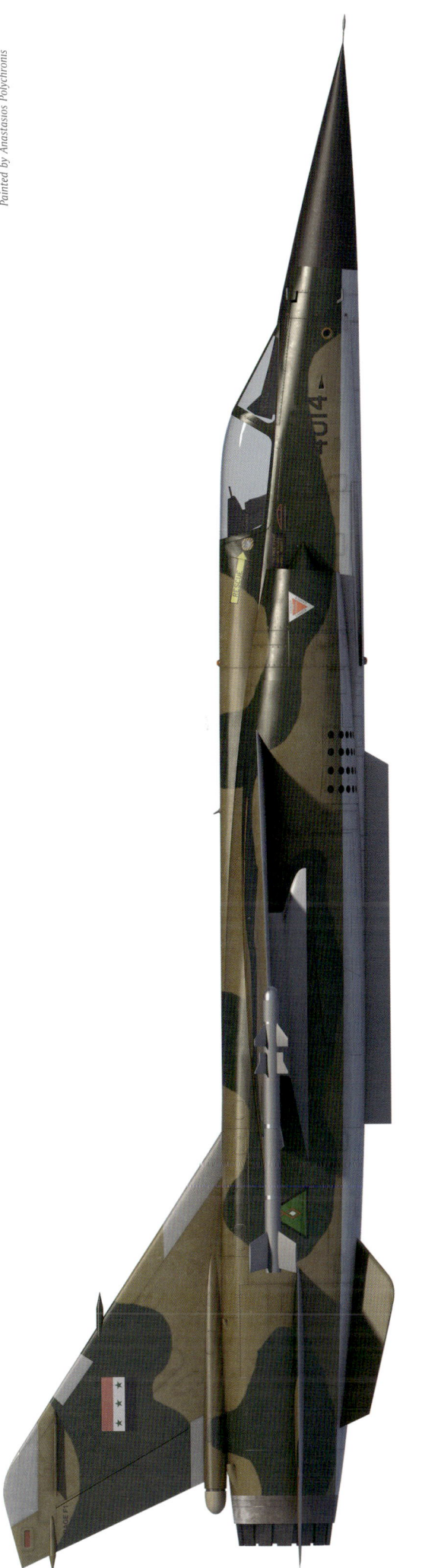

4014 of 79th Squadron, Iraqi Air Force, January 1982

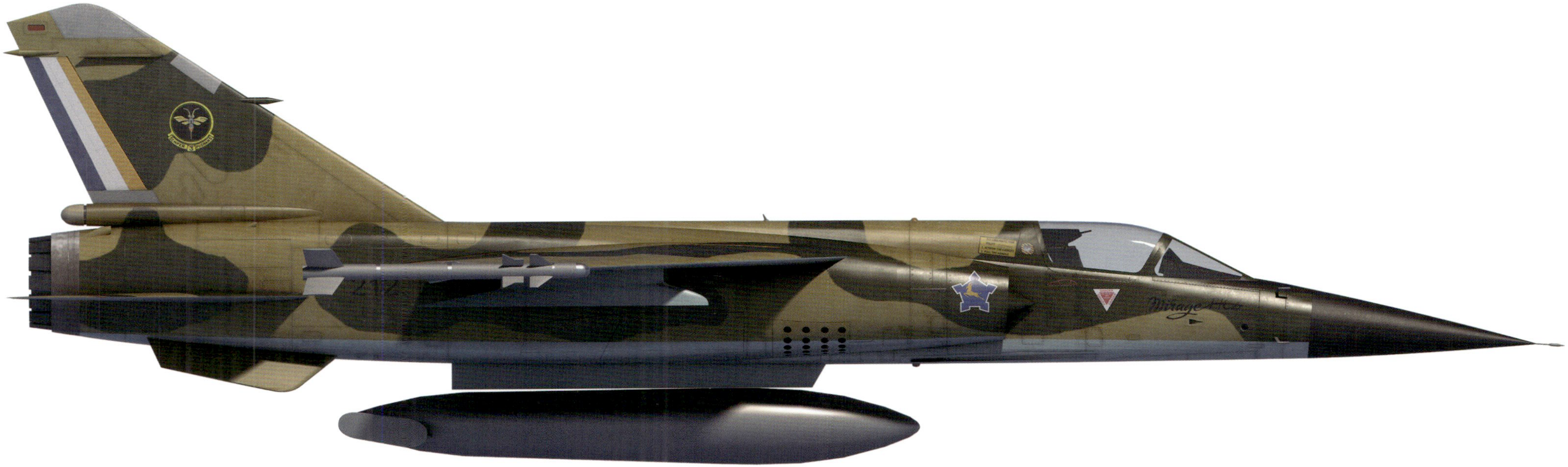

212 of 3rd Squadron, SAAF, 1985

121 of 114 PM, Hellenic Air Force, 2003

8052 of 25th Squadron, Royal Jordanian Air Force

Painted by Anastasios Polychronis